Bridging the Bond

The Cultural Construction
of the Shelter Pet

TAMI L. HARBOLT

Purdue University Press
West Lafayette, Indiana

Library of Congress Cataloging-in-Publication Data
Harbolt, Tami L., 1969-
 Bridging the bond : the cultural construction of the shelter pet /
Tami L. Harbolt.
     p. cm.
Includes bibliographical references and index.
 ISBN 1-55753-260-5 (cloth : alk. paper)
 1. Animal welfare. 2. Animal shelters. 3. Pets. I. Title.
 HV4708 .H373 2002
 636.08´32—dc21
                          2002012969

"In a sense, committed writers are the ones who write both to awaken to the consciousness of their guilt and to give their readers a guilty conscience."

—Trinh T. Minh-ha, *Woman, Native, Other*, 10

Contents

Foreword

We humans are not only a social species, but also a nurturing and caring collective. We rescue not only people in need, but land in need of protection and the wildlife within it. The first organized society to protect urban animals dates back to 1866. This organization, New York's American Society for the Prevention of Cruelty to Animals (ASPCA) originally focused on protecting urban horses, and the workers were almost exclusively male. In 1869, women concerned for household pets established the Women's SPCA of Pennsylvania, the first shelter for city dogs and cats. Today, urban humane societies handle mostly dogs and cats.

Society in general is ambivalent towards its humane societies and animals shelters. On the one hand, society often holds shelter workers in contempt for catching and often killing unwanted pet animals; and on the other hand, we do not actively support social policies that would deem these activities unnecessary. While shelter personnel are considered almost saintly for their selfless dedication, they do not get the financial or moral support they deserve. They are often ridiculed and receive very low pay for strenuous and, at times, dangerous work. The activities of the animal shelter are often shrouded in secrecy, in part because the workers may feel unwelcome and in part because we do not really want to know what goes on in an animal shelter.

Tami Harbolt studied the life of the animal shelter worker not just as a student of folklore, but also as a full-time shelter employee, where she worked her way through the ranks. Harbolt combines her personal memoirs with interviews and astute observations of the shelter culture. We learn to appreciate the shelter employee, volunteer, educator, activist, and even pet.

Rarely do people understand one of society's must elusive activities, the animal shelter. But shelters are part of our lives and we should understand them. Tami Harbolt's story is both informative and personal. It takes us through her journey with her own canine and human companions as she navigates a life trying to balance protecting animals and society. She helps us understand a life that tries to treat animals humanely in a world that is sometimes anything but.

—Alan M. Beck
Dorothy N. McAllister Professor of Animal Ecology,
Purdue University

Acknowledgments

This narrative is because of Camille, and therefore is written as a dedication to those qualities that characterized our bond—a desire for mutual protection, unconditional love and completion. In addition, I would like to thank the following people for donating time, energy, and support to this project. Obviously, I need to thank all of the animals, employees, and volunteers of the various shelters and rescue organizations in New Mexico and Kentucky who contributed to this project. Some of them are named in this book, but far more have come and gone and may have thought no one noticed the small acts of kindness, and sometimes callousness, that they performed in my presence. Most of all, I want to thank the thousands and thousands of animals I have met who will also remain nameless in this book. So many of them were so important to someone, and many of them were important to no one. For me, I was only happy to give them a hug, a fresh bowl of water, or a treat at the end of the day. There were *so many* over the course of five years.

There are quite a few young people growing to be future providers—my wonderful Camp, YDDC, and JHA kids—you have been good friends and I hope your paths are always full of triumph and wagging tails. You kept me laughing and made me proud. Tamara Ward, Kim and Chris at Three Dog Bakery—keep up the good work you do. Thanks for making my last year in New Mexico worth a good laugh.

For enthusiasm, guidance, and support, thanks go to Ruth Salvaggio, M. Jane Young, Vera Norwood, and Alan Beck. Without your support of this research, I would not be here writing this now. Without the words—verbal or written—each of you has contributed, I would not have found the courage to pursue a study of animals. I truly appreciate your good humor, knowledge, and stories. Minrose and Ruth—thanks for giving me access to the flavor of southern comfort every now and then and for inspiring me to follow my heritage and be a Southern writer.

For encouraging me to pursue this research long before I knew where it would take me, thanks to Erika Brady, Lynwood Montell, Jay Mechling, Stanley Costello, Marty Vowels, Terry Barrett, Joel Royalty, and Ken Carstens. Dale Leys—I didn't change what I drew, I just changed *how* I drew it. Marty—who knew those stories in the eighth grade would lead to this? With the greatest admiration, Stanley—you were the best teacher I have ever known, and I only hope I can begin to approach your ability to make history a storyteller's canvas.

Although this work has kept me away for far too long, I owe my family appreciation for allowing me to forge my own path and for letting me know I can always come back home. I can't wait to be a real aunt to the babies—Rachel, Tyler, Marco, Carly, Laura, and Scott. Dad—you are you and I am me and I love you. Mom, thanks for confirming my destiny by playing records late at night and teaching me your decorating style. Paw-paw and Mom-mom—thanks for the gift certificates to Cracker Barrel. Michelle and Brooks, Linda and Todd, Rick, Aunt Dot and Uncle Morrie, Valerie—thanks for being wonderful, intelligent role models. Becky, thanks for Danny. Amy and Sara—once again, I am very proud of you both. Shelly—you are my chosen sister, time after time.

Special thanks to the friends and peers from Western, Murray, and University of New Mexico for letting me chew your ears about these discoveries and for offering an outsider's viewpoint on many of these academic and practical issues. Those of you who gladly braved the fur and wet noses at our house, I hope you realize how happy we all were to see you! Thanks to Paul Malin for helping me live with Murphy a little longer. Dave—you are a hell'a good friend—fried chicken anytime. Debbie—glad we made it. Ila and Mark—don't pin the funk on me, but in the meantime, keep dancing and kicking ass (WWXD?). Lane—thanks for those cocktails. Becca—my health buddy, thanks for those ambulance rides in the Volvo. Jane—good folks are hard to find—glad we found each other in Room 313 Ortega Hall. Anna and Chris—keep on trekking.

I couldn't have completed this without constant reminders and interruptions from Tony, Archie, Curtis, Murphy, Pearl, and Drew. And finally, to my dearest friend and the other mother to all my animals, thanks to Rutledge. The lives of many animals were drawn into our story. Their futures were surely helped along by full bellies, amoxicillin, and premature housebreaking. I have treasured every moment we shared, just as I have treasured every life we saved together. Though we lost a few of them (sweet Carmen, Kismet, little Beatrice), hopefully most of them, like Dale, will get to see a ripe old age. And in my old age, I will remember these years as some of the best I have known. Keep in mind, the hounds of love are always hunting.

I would like to extend my deepest gratitude to my friends and collaborators at Purdue University Press. Margaret, your phone call on September 27 made the happiest day of my life nearly kill me with joy. Andie, I am so grateful to have connected with you through these stories. Once again, Camille is blessing me with her small contributions to life.

BRIDGING THE BOND

Camille's Story

When I decided to get my first dog, my roommate and best friend, Rutledge, who had owned dogs much longer than I had, became so excited for me that I got a little irritated. She was only trying to offer advice, but I felt as if she were trying to pick my dog out for me, and this was a very personal decision. I knew I wanted a Border collie cross (Yes, I was naive!) because I wanted a dog that was intelligent and beautiful. I had seen these dogs perform at obedience trials and was impressed by their focus and drive to please. I went to the nonprofit animal shelter and was turned down because technically our household already owned more animals than the city ordinance allowed. I didn't get anywhere with the adoption counselor when I explained that the dogs belonged to my roommate and that I needed one of my own. So I defiantly started driving to adoption clinics all over town, being careful about how much information I offered the counselors. I knew the other groups called themselves "no-kill," meaning they didn't euthanize animals as they did at the shelter or pound. I also knew they fostered the animals in their homes, which made me imagine that I might get an adult dog that was already housebroken. Other than that, I knew very little about their ideologies or philosophies. Looking back, I also knew very little about dogs. It might have been better if I had taken some of Rutledge's advice, but I was stubborn and determined to choose my dog for myself.

I was cruising along on a shopping trip one day and drove past a veterinarian's office where an adoption clinic was in progress. Out of the corner of my eye, I noticed a little tri-colored dog, so I turned around and went back. There were several dogs there, some on leashes, and some in crates. I stated my interest to the couple in charge of the animals and asked about the little dog I had seen from the street. I was told that she was a special case. She had been abused and would require someone with plenty of time and commitment. I thought she was beautiful. Not only did she have many of the features of a Border collie, she had the coloring of a Bernese mountain dog, one of my other favorite breeds. She had a sharp delicate bone structure, wide round eyes, no tail, and she seemed completely enamored of the woman who was fostering her. They told me her name was Camilla, after a character in a movie called *Camille Claudel* (1990) about a sculptress who was Rodin's student and mistress, and who eventually went mad after he scorned her. What should have been my first warning sounded wildly romantic to me. Here was a tragic little dog that I could care for and perhaps rehabilitate. I remembered watching movies and reading books as a child about girls who found abused dogs and horses and armed with only love, patience, and time, turned them into champions! I was resolved, despite the initial reluctance of the couple to let her go, to take this little dog home with me.

After talking to them for almost two hours, I convinced them that I would take good care of Camilla. It was obvious that the woman was attached to her, and as the afternoon wore on I learned more about the dog's background. They told me they had found her on the street, and it had taken several months to get her home. Once they got her there, it was even longer before she would come inside the house. They had gotten her socialized enough to be adopted out once, but when they went to do a check on her they found her tied out in front of an apartment complex where children were throwing rocks at her. She had been back with them ever since, but the man still couldn't pet her if he looked at her. He had to wait for her to approach him and keep his eyes averted. They asked me if I would be bringing her back to them once I got a boyfriend who didn't like her, and I laughed and explained that in my house, the animals come first. Before I could leave with her they asked me to go home and introduce her to our alpha dog, to be sure there would be no immediate conflicts. Lucy, an Airedale-golden cross, accepted Camilla with hardly a glance, so I signed the contract and paid $40.00 for her spay and shots. When Camilla wouldn't get in the car with me, I handed the leash to Lucy, who pulled her in with the leash between her teeth and I drove them home.

When Rutledge came home from work, all she said was, "You got a dog." I told her Camille's story (I shortened her name right away) and explained why she wouldn't allow Rutledge to pet her. I told her I was going to rehabilitate her, and Rutledge said, 'Well, OK!' I could see she had her doubts. Already Camille was hiding under the couch, and she would scamper away if I opened a garbage bag, shook a newspaper, or used a broom, brush, or any other object that a person might use on an animal. The first night she lived there, she peed on the living room floor right in front of me, after I had stood outside for about an hour telling her to "go potty." Later that night, the cats cornered her and beat her up. Not a good start!

Three nights later, after I came home from work, Camille had a seizure. I was alone, and I had never seen a dog have a seizure, so I called my veterinarian, hysterical that I had accidentally poisoned her. Luckily, he made house calls and he arrived in fifteen minutes. By then the seizure was over, and he told me that her condition was treatable, and asked pointedly if I would be keeping her. Although I was angry that the foster family had not informed me of this, I told him that there was no question that I would be keeping her. We decided to wait to start treatment until after we determined how frequent and intense her epilepsy actually was.

Over the course of the next six months, I worked at getting Camille to trust me. Every day after work, I walked her. At first she tried sleeping in my roommate's room with her dogs, so I started crating her in my room. The crating also came about because I was sure she was *not* housebroken, despite the assurances from the foster family that she was. So far, she had already repeatedly marked the carpeted areas of the house and had ruined a rug. When I tried to discipline her for her transgressions, she ran and hid under the couch. We blocked off the couch and put plastic under the rugs. I also learned that I couldn't keep her in the house alone because she suffered from separation anxiety. She had nearly knocked out a window trying to get out of the house. As a renter, these were chances I could not take. She rummaged through the garbage, and several times peed on my bed if I left her alone in my room. Living in the southwest allows for dry and pleasant weather nearly all year round, so from that point on Camille stayed outside when I wasn't home. Not that this was a foolproof plan, because it took me about two months to completely secure the yard to guarantee that she could not climb or dig under fences. I caught her outside of the yard one day when I came home unexpectedly, and I still wonder how many times she managed to go for a stroll and then beat me home.

She also had a problem with men, which I had known about when I got her, but wasn't really prepared for. When male friends visited we advised them *never* to enter the yard without one of us being there. Camille still managed to bite about four people the first year I had her, including my landlord. Luckily, none of these bites were too severe, usually located in the calf, in keeping with her herding instincts. Many times she executed these bites when she believed that these men were advancing towards me suspiciously.

There *were* improvements in her behavior. She decided that I was okay, especially considering the walk deal, and she started letting me pet and brush her. After a while she even started cuddling up with me on the bed. Her obedience training was easy after she decided to bond with me; she loved going for walks and took no time at all to learn to sit, stay, lie down, and heel. It was a game to her, and it made me acutely aware of her intelligence. Her favorite game was when I would tell her to sit, drop the leash, and walk away. If I stopped suddenly and swung around, there she would be, right behind me, slinking forward, like she was whispering "Shhhh . . ." and walking on her tippy toes. As soon as I caught her she would sit down and her mouth would open into a wide grin. I couldn't correct her of this very successfully because I had to laugh with her. This humor, though a bit crazed, was what made me start to fall in love with her and actually enjoy her company.

Her seizures continued over this time, and after one lasted about two hours I decided it was time to get her checked out. Instead of calling my regular veterinarian, I decided to take her back to the clinic where I had adopted her, thinking that they would have her history and understand her behavioral problems. Let me remind you that while I was able to pet her, she still wouldn't let me hug her or pick her up. Any type of physical proximity had to be on her terms, but I figured that the people at the clinic should understand this when I told them where she had come from. That afternoon, to my surprise, they rushed into the office where we sat waiting, scooped Camille off the floor onto the examination table, and immediately put her into a restraining hold in order to draw blood. I tried to explain that she was a rescued dog and to be careful, but as I was trying to say this, Camille turned to bite the technician. I walked up to my dog and started stroking her head, telling her it would be all right.

The technician let her go, turned to me and said, "Don't you tell her it's all right! It is not all right for her to bite me!"

I was stunned. As soon as the technician left I regained my composure and demanded that the veterinarian justify the rudeness of her technician. I was there, paying them *my* money to examine an abused dog, and they were telling me to "shut up!" The veterinarian explained that they were often bitten in their line of work, and that usually it was the owner's fault. It didn't seem to matter to her what Camille's life story was. As far as she was concerned this was just another bad dog, and more than likely the dog was a biter because of something I had done to her. I told her I would have been perfectly happy to muzzle Camille, had they only asked me before they started working on her. That night, after a good cry, I called the main veterinarian in the office, voiced my complaints, and then immediately called my regular veterinarian back in. He was perfectly willing to work with her and me, and he did so over the next five years. Once he even checked her out without her muzzle!

We started her on phenobarbital to treat the epilepsy. The sedative worked at reducing the frequency and severity of her seizures, and, frankly, it helped with some of her behavioral problems as well. There was always a small window when we had to increase the dosage and she would be falling off of furniture and running into walls—but she didn't bite anybody else, I never caught her out of the yard again, and she seemed somewhat more relaxed than before. I started becoming hopeful that with the pheno and time, she might eventually become a normal, happy dog. She even seemed to enjoy taking the medication, as if she knew that it made her feel better. Perhaps she did know.

During this time, my application to graduate school was accepted to the program in American studies, so I quit my full-time job and started working part-time at the animal shelter. Some days I took Camille to work and she hid under my desk all day. My co-workers were kind to her and didn't approach her without asking permission. Only once was there an incident. A volunteer approached my desk and reached down to pet her. Camille promptly gave her a warning snap. The volunteer said "Where did this horrible little dog come from?" I looked at her and said, "She's my dog—a rescue dog." The volunteer raised her eyebrows and walked away. Despite some of her advances, Camille still didn't trust strangers. She still had seizures and worst of all, she still wasn't housebroken. I also found out more about her background when the couple I got her from was found living in the mountains in a trailer with over sixty animals in various stages of neglect and starvation. When employees at our shelter and local authorities confiscated the animals, stories circulated that the woman was found walking around the trailer in her bare feet, with at least an inch of feces covering the floors, walls, countertops, and beds. These cases of inadvertent neglect are common in the sheltering field—people with the best of intentions start sheltering animals to avoid having them euthanized, and quickly find that they have taken on more than they can handle. At least in this case, most of the animals were well socialized and happy, but it was no wonder Camille had never been housebroken! And chances are, with sixty other animals to deal with, the couple may not have even been aware that Camille had epilepsy.

The case of the animal hoarding prompted a discussion between myself and one of my co-workers regarding the difference between *quality* of life and *quantity* of life. I had long accepted the philosophy that it was necessary to euthanize healthy animals, if for no other reason than to avoid any future suffering in a world where there are simply not enough good homes available. The question we were stuck with was, How do you teach other people that quality of life is a more reasonable goal? What was the answer to pet overpopulation, horrible neglect, and abuse, other than merciful death?

After I finished my coursework and final compositions, I decided to move home to Kentucky. Knowing that Camille would be separated from my roommate's dogs, I got another puppy to keep her company. Drew came into my life through a homeless person who found her walking down the street with a chain and padlock around her tiny neck. Although I was in denial that she was a pit bull for the first several months, she immediately settled into our pack and was housebroken in only two weeks. Camille seemed to accept her, but one day I had to rescue Drew from her jaws when Camille attacked her over a rawhide. She left the puppy with several punctures in her face and neck, but Drew quickly grew up with the ability to take care of herself in any similar situation. Rutledge and I could see that Drew had the self-confidence to be an alpha dog after Lucy passed on, and we could also see that eventually Camille would accept this hierarchy.

That May I moved home to Kentucky with two cats and my two dogs; I was nervous about moving in with my father. He had wall-to-wall white carpet and a low fence, and I knew I would have to work longer hours and leave Camille at home. I would have to leave her in the house because the weather at home was not quite so conducive to leaving a dog outside. We secured the fence and I started crating Camille again. I found a job that split my hours so that I could drive home and let her out of the crate in the middle of the day, which I did, despite the fact that the drive was a half an hour each way. I didn't socialize much, considering that I had to be home twice a day to dose her. My roommate had been the only other person Camille would let close enough to stick those pills down her throat. Despite my dad's patience with her, she still spooked easily if he moved towards her too fast.

I can't deny that she adored me, and that's why I tolerated her behavior and literally rearranged my life around her. She followed me all

over the house, was ecstatic as soon as I walked in the door, and was unin-
terested in anybody else if I was in the room. She was like a little shadow,
creeping behind me wherever I went. I got used to feeling her cold, wet
nose on the back of my leg. Her obsessive pacing and energy were almost
a comfort to me after our five years together, and I was not exactly the most
relaxed person myself. I got used to her following me everywhere—wearing a groove into the floor as we both paced and worried and fidgeted.

After seven months, I moved back to the Southwest to teach a
course on animal rights. As usual before any move, I started worrying
about our living arrangements. The house I moved into had carpet, so I
had to crate her again. It didn't have a high fence, so I couldn't leave her
outside. My landlord informed me that as soon as I left the house,
Camille would start barking, and she would bark away most of the day.
Drew was fine wherever she went—she would sooner die than defecate
or urinate in the house, and she had outgrown her chewing when she
was about a year old.

Something happened to me that year. I faced new challenges in
my professional life, which inevitably led to revelations about my personal
life. My new confidence at work and school made me realize that I was the
only person I knew how to take care of, and that I wasn't responsible for
fixing old broken relationships with family, friends, or lovers. I started to
grow up and grow into myself. Going back home made me aware of what
I had learned living on my own 1,500 miles from my family. I was more
confident and self-assured than I ever had been in my life. I wasn't easily
deterred from difficult tasks, but I also started to understand what I was
able to change and what I had to accept. I was nearly finished with my doc-
toral degree; I was presenting papers at conferences and receiving encouraging feedback; I was teaching, and still working at the shelter. At that
point, I was offered an opportunity to start a pilot program in education at
the shelter and decided to extend my stay to try it.

I had already started questioning my relationship with Camille,
but over the course of that year I actually considered what I could do about
it. I was living in apartments and probably would be for many more years.
I wanted to explore new relationships and challenge myself further by trav-
eling and improving my standard of living. I was tired of cleaning up her
messes. Planning each day around her frustrated me and I realized that I
was stuck with a horrible dilemma. It stayed in the back of my mind, but
I still couldn't bring myself to face the only course of action available to us.
I still had hope that we could somehow work it all out.

For several years, Rutledge and I—once again roommates—had fostered a number of animals from the shelter. These were usually under-age or underweight kittens or pups with kennel cough who needed a safe place to develop or heal. In our other house we had been able to separate the dogs from the animal babies so that they were safe and unharmed. In our new place it was virtually impossible.

The first dead kitten was hard to pin on any pet, despite the knowledge that only one of them had ever shown any aggressive tenden-cies toward smaller animals. Although all of the dogs seemed hypersensi-tive the day we found the kitten, we chose to call it "an accident" and vowed to never leave the dogs unsupervised with foster kittens again.

Nonetheless, in my heart I knew which dog had done it. I started thinking more seriously about what I would do with her. I talked to my co-workers, who, when I told them the extent of her history of behavioral problems, couldn't believe I had tolerated her so long. They asked me why I was trying to save a dog that was beyond help, especially when there were so many healthy dogs who needed good homes and good owners. Healthy dogs, they reminded me needlessly, that were euthanized every day in the place we worked. I replied that it was love, and all the work I had done, that she was beautiful and sweet. I couldn't forfeit all the sacrifices I had made. That kept me from making the decision to end her life. Even though I knew, and they reminded me, that I had given her more time and more love than most of the people in the world would have, I still couldn't make a decision like that based only on my comfort and convenience. She was relatively healthy except for the epilepsy, and could probably live out her natural life with the aid of the medication. Still, I found myself becoming more disenchanted with her and drawn to Drew's lazy, low-key approach to life. It was a stark contrast to Camille's frenetic overload. I also realized that Camille had probably reached the plateau of her rehabilitation, and that her behavior was as good as it was going to get. To hope for any more improvements was self-defeating and unreasonable.

That July we were fostering several underage kittens. While I was at work, my roommate discovered one of them, a tiny calico we had named Saavedra, dead. It was obvious that Camille had committed the act. None of the other dogs would look at her or go near her. They knew that this was a sin in our house, and they promptly shunned her from the pack. When I got home ten minutes later, I found Rutledge carrying the dead kit-ten through the house, crying. She kept telling me she hated Camille, even though she knew it was unreasonable, and that she couldn't help it. I sat down outside, lit a cigarette, and called my veterinarian. I told him it was time, but he couldn't make it to the house for another couple of days. Since I had two days off work, I decided I wouldn't wait. I called the shelter and spoke to my friend who was kennel manager and an expert at euthanasia. She told me to bring her up right away. I made arrangements at the crematorium and we loaded Camille in the car.

At about 3:00 p.m. on Saturday, July 3, 1999, I held Camille for the last time. Rutledge was there with us, and my friend and co-worker administered the solution. There was only one second when I hesitated and wondered once more if I was doing the right thing. Then the needle was in, and in seconds she was gone. For the first time in her life, I felt her shoulders relax. She stared straight ahead as she lay on the metal table and I tried closing her eyes. I asked everyone to leave the room for a while and I sobbed into her dusty, sleek coat. Then my friend came back in and opened a garbage bag for her. I noticed that she had also been crying. She had put one of her cats down only a few weeks before, and she said; "Now Camille and Beetlejuice are together." I found Rutledge outside on the steps, still holding the dead kitten and still sobbing. After affectionately admonishing her to place the poor kitten in the freezer until we could bury it, I carried Camille to the car and we drove to the crematorium.

On the way there, a song came on the radio— Sarah McLachlan's "Angel" (1997), about a woman who suffers from addiction and dies alone in a hotel room. The chorus of the song relays the singer's hope that the woman finds herself in the arms of the angels, at last in peace and comfort:

> It don't make no difference, escape one last time. It's easier to believe in this sweet madness, oh this glorious sadness that brings me to my knees.

> You're in the arms of the angels, fly away from here from this dark cold hotel room and the endlessness that you fear. You are pulled from the wreckage of your silent reverie. You're in the arms of the angels, may you find some comfort here.   .
> (McLachlan 1997)

As we listened to a haunting version sung live by McLachlan and Emmylou Harris, to Rutledge and me it seemed as if the universe was sending us a message that we had made the right choice. At that moment, any doubts I had about my decision were subdued. Even though the body in the backseat was still, I knew that Camille and I had been equally blessed to know one another, that she was grateful I had entered her life, and that she forgave me for ending it. Wherever she was, her pain and continual fear had ended. Her inhabitance of her frail body was over, but she would never be gone from my heart.

Later, it occurred to me that Camille's life had provided me with an infinite resource for my research and answers in my personal and spiritual life as well. In the years that she lived with me, she provided me with insight into the world of rescuing and sheltering animals, about the limits of sacrifice and the boundaries of caring. She helped me realize what had motivated me to pursue this area of research, and, based on my life experiences, why I was uniquely suited to work in an animal shelter. The comments and advice I received from people regarding her life and death ran the full course of philosophies and beliefs and actions regarding the care of pets in our culture—the responsibility we have towards the domestic animals with whom we share our lives. Our culture has often been characterized as one that disregards the sanctity of life. Violence against children, women, the environment, the elderly, and the mentally ill are all symptoms of some perceived undercurrent of moral disease that pervades our popular and traditional culture. And yet I have met a number of individuals who believe that they can make some small differences in the lives of individual animals (and by virtue of that association, other people) that make the world a kinder, more humane place for all. Their reasons for helping animals are not only motivated by a strong sense of nurturing, but often by a spiritual connection to other creatures in this world, especially creatures with very little power or control over their own lives. These people understand that just as there is sanctity for life, there is also a sacred element to death—that there are connections, and not necessarily only endings.

Many who read this may question my decision to end Camille's life. Since I had her euthanized, I have analyzed my decision myself. Some have asked why I chose the foster kittens over my dog of five years, or why I couldn't find her another home. Some have said nothing with words, but have turned away from the discussion and left me feeling vaguely troubled and guilty. I cannot deny that I participate in a culture that often views death as the only alternative for some animals. In addition, I have participated in a subculture that specifically kills animals for whom it cannot find adequate homes. Perhaps there was someone who would have been willing to take Camille in and allow her to live out her natural life. I am not a person who readily trusts the good intentions of well-meaning individuals, and after five years of knowing her, I was not about to put her or anyone else through that transition. There are also those who believe that I did more than was reasonable to try to rehabilitate her. These are the individuals who believe that the goal of an animal welfarist should be to prevent suffering, not prolong life. These are slippery issues, and they require more contemplation and morality than I can even begin to approach in this examination. Does good "health" encompass mental health when it comes to our pets? Are some behavioral problems adequate reasons for death? Once again, it is an issue of quality, and different people have far differing opinions on how to achieve this. These are issues that cannot be determined by one individual or group. I will state that the decisions to surrender an animal, either to a rescue or welfare organization or to death, are not always easy ones to make. Quite often, they incorporate an individual's life history, current lifestyle and circumstances, and moral beliefs about the value of animal life. Animals are woven into our lives in ways that we seldom consider and infrequently acknowledge. The stories I will retell in this volume are not only about animals or just about people—they are stories about *the bond*, the connection between species that makes our lives as social creatures possible. They are stories about how a group of people *bridge* that permanent bond by constructing animal lives with thoughts, actions, and philosophies, and how the animals recover (or not) from those expectations. It is that warm and mysterious space between us— commonly called empathy— which allows for communication and exploration upon which I will focus.

This book will cover the observations and conversations from the five years I spent working in animal shelters. It is a cultural ethnography, a memoir, and a series of essays regarding the experience of rejected pets in a typical American urban environment. Chapter 1 will introduce the conflicts and set the stage, as well as present the tools, both personal and professional, I employed to study the relationships between homeless animals and their caretakers. Chapters 2 and 3 will discuss the historical roots of the animal welfare movement, the cultural construction of pet keeping, and the history of contemporary welfare groups on national and local levels. Chapter 4 will introduce the reader to the people who work with these animals, either as volunteers or employees at shelters and rescue groups. This section will focus on the goals, motivations, frustrations, and triumphs of the day-to-day care of abandoned pets. In Chapter 5, I will construct the identity of the shelter pet by examining the incorporation of an animal into a shelter and by focusing on specific animals that made significant impacts on workers in these environments. I will show that although workers incorporate a great deal of institutional learning and personal experience, influenced at times by popular or traditional beliefs about animals, there are animals who resist construction and act in ways that defy categorization in this culture. Other animals, through incorporation, become perfect examples of the "constructed" shelter or rescued pet, fulfilling the expectations of the people involved in the rescue and rehabilitation of the animal. The next section will describe the ethnographic and theoretical tools others have provided me to approach the study of animals.

How to Approach a Strange Dog

Examining the animal's perspective can do more than merely enlarge the corpus of sociological [or any] theory and method. A far broader and ultimately more important goal is to counter the masculinist, positivist, structuralist, reductionist view of the natural world and the place of "man" within it. *Interpretive-experiential involvement in the exchange between people and animals provides an opportunity to reconstruct the world of nature* [italics mine]. (Arluke and Sanders 1996, 56–57)

When an animal enters a shelter, it is, quite often, reluctant. Usually, it is one of the only times the animal has been outside of the familiar environment he knew as home, or prior to coming to the shelter has only been to the veterinarian. It is common for a dog to plant all four feet firmly onto the concrete sidewalk and refuse to cross the threshold. If a worker isn't already busy with another animal or telephone call, she may walk over to the door to nudge the dog in from behind. Extremely scared and obstinate dogs are simply dragged in at the end of the leash. This sometimes seems harsh to those observing the interaction from afar, but a dog who bites a person before he gets inside is sent to Animal Control, where they possess the equipment to handle vicious and snappy dogs. Once the dog has crossed the threshold, there are a number of behaviors he may exhibit. Some cringe behind the legs of the person bringing him in. Seldom do workers approach such an animal until after crucial information is obtained from the person relinquishing it. Some dogs wag their tails, jump on everyone in the room, tug at the leash, whine and pace around when they see the resident cats, and graciously accept the token treat offered by a volunteer. A few dogs lift their legs, much to the embarrassment of the owners who just claimed, unequivocally, that the dogs were housebroken. Occasionally a dog will lunge in an attempt to take the arm off of the closest stranger.

The introduction does not stop there. After an initial observation by experienced staff, a worker will approach the dog in order to tag him and check for age and gender. This is when the communication between a shelter worker and an animal is established. Experienced workers know to squat on the floor so that they are on the same level as the dog (this only applies to dogs—cats are a whole different process). They avoid direct eye contact, often looking down at the floor or over at a wall. If the dog has made no move to bite, the worker will slowly extend an open hand, typically with a treat at the tip of her fingers. The next move belongs to the dog. If

An incoming dog at AHANM

he approaches, even shyly, he is almost always accepted. The worker resumes a dominant posture by reaching over the dog's head to apply a temporary collar, and at this time trusts that she can make eye contact with the dog. After gazing at the dog for only a few seconds, the worker gives the dog a name if he doesn't already have one, and determines the dog's age and gender. After the worker conducts an interview with the relinquishing human, the dog is dragged, carried, or walked back to the processing kennel with a computer generated number, a kennel card, and, possibly, a new name. His identity as a shelter pet is established.

The process by which a worker first communicates with a strange animal involves more than just understanding technique and behavioral response. Sometimes, the identity of a shelter pet begins to evolve as soon as an owner or finder calls to tell the worker that she is bringing the animal in. This identity continues to evolve over the course of the animal's stay in a shelter. The name, the breed designation, the description placed on a kennel card, the cage he is placed in, the home he will be sent to (or not) and the personality of the pet—all are determined by a process that involves each individual who has any contact with the animal, as well as the actual behaviors and expressions the animal exhibits. Just as I learned, over time, how to approach and handle strange animals, I have developed a method and approach to the study of human-animal interactions. This chapter will discuss the tools, both technical and intuitive, I found most valuable in achieving the goal of representing humans (including myself) and non-humans in my work. My goal is to recreate some aspects of the world of animal welfare work for the reader. I will base this reconstruction on findings in previous research, the narratives I have gathered from other workers, the events found in historical documentation, and my experiences and observations of the handling, incorporation, and behaviors of companion animals in shelter and rescue environments.

I plan to elaborate on the research of other social scientists to allow for a more detailed analysis of the shelter and rescue environment. I believe that a more interpretive-experiential method has allowed for the voices of both the workers and the animals, as past ethnographies have not. It would be wrong, however, to read this book and expect a strictly ethnographic approach, or an anthropological treatment, or even a purely literary description of the environment. I have joyfully included my own experiences here in an effort to make it as real and rich for the reader as possible. It would be most appropriate to describe this as a *cultural study of the animal shelter environment.*

When I originally presented portions of my research on animal euthanasia at an academic conference, a woman in the audience asked me a provocative question about the role of self-disclosure in research writing. I was employing a method that did not remove feelings or emotions from my work, and although this method has been employed by feminist researchers, it still makes people (especially academics) uncomfortable. Add to that the fact that I was talking about killing animals, and my subject was nearly impossible to discuss without some melodrama and intensity. The audience member stated that she was familiar with experimental ethnographies, but that she usually found some of them "kind of whiny." She wondered whether I was concerned with presenting myself in such a light by offering personal narratives in academic pieces. I nearly laughed out loud, but managed to keep my mirth hidden behind a grin when I said, "All of the time!" I had struggled constantly with how to discuss material that lent itself easily to romanticization and sentimentality. I can recognize the difference between a popular treatment of the subject matter and a sociological perspective, and I could, if I wanted to, employ either approach. Like anyone else, I was afraid to open myself up to explore the feelings that motivated me as a participant and a researcher, even though I knew I didn't want to present it in such a way that portrayed me as unfeeling and disconnected from my subjects. When talking about animals, I was by no means objective or distant.

And when I delivered a paper at the conference that discussed the process by which I became indoctrinated at a shelter that kills animals, I opened myself up to a fair amount of criticism and left the audience feeling uncomfortable and drained. After I read the first sentence, "The first time I witnessed a killing. . .," there were people who left the room. I later learned that they had left because this particular subject was too difficult for them. I would only exacerbate their discomfort by discussing my own feelings throughout the essay, not allowing them to distance themselves from the reality of my experience by relaying the message in safe, academic discourse. My style of writing has developed over years of conscious consideration, and a personal, literary style allows me to communicate my message (and of course I have one!) to people who are typically unaccustomed to reading academic texts (which would be the majority of my human subjects). It has been a primary concern of mine, ever since I entered academia as a psychology major, to make my work immediately accessible and meaningful to the people identified in my writing. Whatever sacrifice this brings about in terms of legitimacy among academics has been a risk I wholeheartedly take. My goal is to stimulate research, writing, and discussion, as much as it is to uncover a perspective not previously considered.

My personal experiences working in an animal shelter for the past several years have led me to believe that people are drawn to sheltering work out of more than simply a desire to help animals. Many of the people I met in this community had experienced various forms of oppression, either in a familial, societal, or biological way. This experience of oppression led many of these workers and volunteers to develop a heightened empathy for animals, based on the perceived experience of shared oppression and suffering. While these experiences may have reinforced the idea of animals as victims, there are often times in these environments when animals exhibit and express individual characteristics, personalities, and desires. Workers, who come to the work with what could be thought of as a "touch" for animals, further develop their skills to share a communication with these animals. Similarly, the animals themselves come into a shelter with a wide variety of interspecies communicative skills, some adaptive, and some not. Similarly, some of the shelter workers also exhibit some inconsistencies in adaptive behaviors, and working with animals often heightens these behaviors.

I will suggest in this book that people are drawn to animal shelter and welfare work because it is highly dramatic, intense, and characterized by joyful highs and overwhelming setbacks. And it satisfies some need in people, not only to control their social environments, but also to rearrange their legacies of disenfranchisement. Obviously, I am basing some of this hypothesis on my own "legacy of disenfranchisement" and how animals have empowered me. I have heard the director at the shelter say many times, "The people that work in this business wear their hearts on their sleeves." Essentially, he was telling me that melodrama is unavoidable. Indeed, it becomes apparent, after only a few days in an animal shelter, that people who care very deeply for animals surround you, and their commitment to them sometimes has severe effects on their relationships with other people.[1] By this statement, I am not suggesting, as is commonly implied, that "animal-people" can't also be "people-people." I am suggesting that the qualities associated with service work that include self-sacrifice, rescuing, and intense emotional commitment are more than satisfied in this line of work, and may even be exacerbated by virtue of the fact that the victims are considered voiceless and powerless members of our communities.

The workers in these environments have the responsibility of representing the needs of verbally restricted members of our social and cultural worlds. None of these workers would accept the statement that "animals can't talk." They would counter this accusation with the statement "Most people don't know how to listen." People who work with animals understand that animals *speak* and that a communication is exchanged. Unfortunately, this form of communication is not adequate to prevent mistreatment, neglect, and disregard for the welfare of this population. Just as Bernard Rollin has suggested, if animals could not feel pain, then they would not be used as subjects in experiments studying pain (1989). If they did not respond to the infliction of cruelty by yelping and whining, they would not be abused, just as other nondominant members of our society are abused. Those people most commonly represented as interpreters of this language, as the historical documentation of the animal welfare movement will suggest, are individuals who have often themselves experienced some form of social disenfranchisement. According to most research, 80 percent of the people in the animal rights movement are women (Peek et al. 1986). Women occupy a category of social disenfranchisement that brings about a need to reconstruct their social worlds in sometimes subversive and nonthreatening ways. Animal sheltering is one of those sites of social reconstruction.

Just as women have for centuries centered their inquiries of the natural and social world in the form of letters, journals, children's stories, and illustrations (Gates and Schtier 1997), I will incorporate the personal anecdote and rely on a personal knowledge of the "subjects" in question. Much of the information I present will be in the form of anecdotal stories, which I feel are relevant to many of the issues confronting animal welfare workers. Dramatic narratives, punctuated by exaggeration, lyricism, formulaic endings and intertwined with other common cultural narratives, will be an aspect of this work that I will not always draw specific attention to during the course of this book. I believe I am representative of a strong theoretical movement in the study of the human-animal bond to include anecdotal information as reasonable scientific study (Rollin 1989, 150–152).

The following day, when I saw the woman who had questioned my use of personal narratives at the conference, I told her, "You know, I don't really *want* you to get too comfortable when I talk about killing animals. It wouldn't be fair to those animals or the people who work there." With that statement, I believe I conveyed more about my method and subject positioning than anything else I had said or written. I never write as an uninvolved, disinterested ethnographer. I am, at all times, involved in changing a deplorable system of handling surplus pets. I am a researcher, an advocate, a writer, a welfarist, a woman, and a shelter worker. All of these identities combine to produce a work such as this one. My primary motive was to write something that humanizes the people that work in shelters where animals are killed. In order to do that, I had to become one of those people. In the process of research and writing, I discovered new aspects of my own sense of well-being and humanity. The irony and inconsistency of studying death to learn about life is obvious and tragic. But I believe if more people are made aware of what happens to pets after they are left at a shelter, then maybe people will reconsider their willingness to participate in, or even merely accept, this system. Perhaps this examination will also allow them to consider the place of pets in the world in general. Our current system of handling pet overpopulation requires that people who care about animals justify a system of killing to prevent suffering. This narrative gave many of the people who alleviate suffering and provide for the deaths of companion animals a chance to articulate their motivations, beliefs, and experiences.

My critique of the system of animal welfare is based on my advocacy of the work. I do not endorse the idea of life at any cost. Sometimes the cost seems too great. I have extended this resistance to the system *while working within that system* to writing and research. The scientific method, as reliable and consistent as its practitioners claim, has resulted in some of the most horrid abuses of animals (humans included) in the course of history. I was moved to approach my research from a new perspective after learning that other writers, mainly those tucked into the general category of cultural studies, were not willing to study science and technology using the same tools. I believe that the methodological issue of "going native," or becoming a member of your research community, is one that illuminates many of these theoretical concerns. Ethnographies written from the perspective of friendship and total participation allow for an attention to detail and subtlety that cannot be obtained by distance and objectivity. Just as a person unfamiliar with the subtle cues that an animal is *speaking* cannot hear the animal, neither can a person unfamiliar with the cues of a culture of which she has no real investment write about it. Friendship and empathy are cornerstones to the ethnography of animals. Although other researchers have suggested that no fieldworker can ever be completely accepted by their (presumably human) subjects, I found that by becoming a member of the subculture I studied, I was fully accepted as a participant. This acceptance reached the point that my subjects often forgot that I was also an observer and writer, even though I reminded them of this fact constantly. My fear was not that they would withhold information from me or change their behavior in my presence, but that they would forget that every incident I observed and participated in could become a story I would retell in my writing. Instead of wondering whether I would have an insider's view of animal sheltering, I was more concerned with which stories would describe the people I worked with in an unflattering light. Nonetheless, I would not have been allowed to participate as fully in certain situations had I not already established myself among my co-workers as worthy of their trust. For example, animal euthanasia is not only a somewhat private event; it is an event that has many layers of meaning—something an outsider could never comprehend after only a few hours of observation. The motivations behind why many of these people worked in the shelter and rescued animals were not things I determined only in tape-recorded interviews, but through the process of developing friendships and peer-ships.

Finally, understanding what companion animals are *saying* does not simply occur just because a researcher happens to own a pet. Each animal is unique in her own ways—some subtle and some more obvious. In turn, each animal produces different reactions and outcomes in these settings. *In a shelter, a dog or cat is nearly stripped of the meanings and definitions with which her owner had represented her. That animal had to learn to "speak" herself, or the workers have to "speak" for her.* In essence, the story of her life is reconstructed. I could only have interpreted these events with a great deal of practical experience. Therefore, I actively employed a "friendship frame" when approaching my fieldwork, relying on "collaboration" and "affiliation" rather than alienation and intellectual distance.

Women's ethnography—and specifically works by authors who have chosen to incorporate themselves into the research environment by subjectifying their positions—has provided me with a roadmap. It has given me a means to bring my personal narrative into play here, to incorporate my story with the stories of the lives that I have followed for the past few years. Acknowledging the risk of losing authority and distance, I have chosen connection and empathy. In doing so, I also risk misrepresenting my subjects, as their experiences are influenced by my own interpretation of events. This is unavoidable in any fieldwork situation. Writing *from* and *about* my position, I hope, will allow the reader to realize that I was aware of this as I listened, asked questions, and retold these stories. As a filter for experience, there are details that will be neglected and events that have been significant only to me, but the alternative, in my opinion, was worse. As writer Patricia Williams asks, "What is 'impersonal' writing, but denial of self? . . . in a world of real others, the cost of such exclusive forms of discourse is empowerment at the expense of one's relation to those others; empowerment without communion" (1991, 92–93).

Trinh T. Minh-ha states: "A conversation of 'us' with 'us' about 'them' is a conversation in which 'them' is silenced" (1989, 67). Personal writing allows for the blending of experience and observation, complete with emotion and reason. I may not always be able to speak for animals, but I can speak as one of those culturally designated as one who speaks for animals. I cannot become another animal, therefore I can never go truly native, but I can explore the closest spaces between us. In the process, I will explore the most striking similarities we possess and the differences that keep us forever on contrasting sides of the species boundary.

I chose to open this book with a story about Camille, as a means of locating my dog and myself in the method of inquiry. Her story was *our* story. On a deeper level, her story has symbolized and encouraged my personal development. Camille's story was also about the many people and animals whose lives she touched: the person or persons who initially abused or neglected her, a "no-kill" foster family, which was eventually cited for animal hoarding, two veterinarians with vastly different approaches to animal welfare and people handling, workers and volunteers at the shelter, family, professors, peers, students, two dead foster kittens, Thor, Lucy, Drew, the cats, and our friends. My own position is inextricably bound with her experience, and her experiences were framed by my structural and ideological position in animal welfare work.

In addition to discussing my own experiences, I conducted twenty-five informal open-ended interviews with employees/volunteers at two animal shelters and three rescue groups. All but one of the subjects interviewed defined themselves as welfarists and not activists, meaning that they were concerned *primarily* with the welfare of companion animals and not with animal rights. There were varying degrees of affiliation with other animal rights philosophies within the sample, from vegetarianism to other forms of animal activism. I chose the subjects based on their level of experience, their willingness to be interviewed, their position within the organization, and their affiliation with specific groups. I interviewed six men and nineteen women. Most of these men were in upper management, and these numbers are roughly the same ratio for the field in general (Peek et al. 1986).

Camille

Photo by Cynthia DeSoto

A small sample size means that these results are not ones that can be precisely replicated by another study. Therefore, there are several variables which have affected the experiences of this particular group of individuals, such as region, ethnicity, level of education, and income, that would make this study subjective rather than "scientific." As I mentioned before, I chose this method based on an intention to collaborate and affiliate, rather than generalize and impersonalize my subjects. Other researchers, who might usually rely on statistical studies of populations, have borrowed more personalized methodologies from other fields, possibly because the population of animal activists, veterinarians, and welfare workers has received so little attention in traditional academic study.

The animals I examined were chosen based on historical significance within the organization and special circumstances. I also chose a few animals randomly to trace the experience of a typical stay in a shelter. Other animals are drawn from my memory or the memories of other workers. Their impact on the lives of these people created detailed narratives that conveyed many messages about the work the people in the organization believed they were accomplishing. These stories were not only told to me, but were told as moral stories to other volunteers and employees as a means of conveying philosophy and mission. Some of these stories had been told and retold so many times that it was apparent the story had been exaggerated and embellished. Perhaps I was the first person to hear the story retold, after the teller had replayed the events a hundred times in his or her mind. Some stories, after we cycle them through our thoughts and feelings, come across to the audience as do dreams after waking. We remember the important parts, forget some of the details, and interpret the data the best we can. The events themselves may even become less significant, or vastly different from the story we are stuck with—the one we believe in and retell. I believe there is a beauty to storytelling that develops as a story becomes the embodiment of an idea or belief about the world. Few of us can deny the allure of stories about the mystery of our bonds with animals and nature. Therefore, I will not always question the veracity of these stories, be they from newspaper accounts, fundraising documents, my informants, or even my own memories. ("The truthfulness of the story, as we already know, does not limit itself to the realm of facts" [Trinh 1989, 144].) In retelling them here in this book, I only mean to note that they give us a sense of how people relate to animals, and how animals in turn recover from our ministrations. Our stories about them affect them in ways we do not always consider. This is the basis of studying how they are constructed through culture. In the course of this book, I will show how the institution of animal welfare creates and sometimes suppresses a "story" about our relationships with animals.

Vicki Hearne, who has written several books on animal emotional and cognitive abilities, states that it was a primary concern of hers to represent animals in ways that were true to their nature, and true to *her experience of them* (Hearne 1982, 3). She is conscious of the need to write about animals in ways that will not be construed as unacceptable, but she also cannot remove the presence of emotion from her relationships with her subjects. Her observations are not clear of her personal biases, and yet I often find her approach more accessible and more truthful than a reliable sample and a clear hypothesis. She writes about animals from her own perspective, and while this means that her findings do not always generalize to others' perceptions, this attempt to be honest about writing allows for a greater depth and complexity.

Hearne recommends that the first fact that must be accepted is that domestic animals are acculturated, and in order to survive, they must learn the rules of human society. Dogs become acculturated through breeding and training (domestication), and this fact proves that there is the presence of communication between species, because training *is a language*. In teaching an animal rules and language, by learning to read their actions and expressions, we are engaged in a communicative act with another species. The act becomes a bond based on a deeper element of this communication:

> Dog and handler, having learned to talk, are now in the presence of and are commanded by love. . . .The dog's apparent command of human language might be limited, but his respect for language commands him now, with his handler, as deeply as only a few poets are commanded. In this sense, command of and by language and respect for language are one.
> (Hearne 1982, 30)

Just as individual animals possess experiences unique to their lives, it is also imperative that we acknowledge that they are socialized, acculturated participants in our culture. This does not imply that their participation is always voluntary, but does suggest that without a bond between people and pets, their lives would have different meanings in relation to our own. The language Vicki Hearne experiences and acknowledges is the language of behavior training. The language this book will discuss, which is common and shared between rejected animals and shelter workers, is the language of *suffering*. The primary themes in that language, as you will see, are those of kindness and cruelty, power and victimization.

By writing about homeless animals in modern America, I am making an attempt to cross boundaries. Through the use of ethnography, reflexive writing, folk studies, and feminist cultural studies I am searching for the point between a graph and a journal entry that will allow me to explore the meanings we construct when we shelter companion animals. In doing so, I hope to offer my own voice as an effective avenue for conveying those meanings and symbols that we share, providing the "voiceless" with an opportunity to convey their subjective positioning. Just as those of us reading this can never truly know absolutely what it means to be a fuzzy, four-legged creature, neither can we assume there are absolutes in studying animals. There is no way for *me* to write a document regarding animal welfare that is value-free and scientifically pure, partly because I do not reasonably believe that those ideals truly exist, and partly because it would be against my nature to do so.

If we are to seek a positive effect of our work, then it is by seeking connection with other creatures, offering them the opportunity to *speak* so that we might understand. This should be the gift of a humane society to all its members. As lawyer and author Patricia Williams states, offering these beings rights, *including the right to speak,* is a gift that adds to our quality of living: "One consequence of this broader reconfiguration of rights is to give a voice to those people, or *things* [italics mine] that, by virtue of their object relation to a contract, historically have no voice . . . [bestowal of rights] increases the limited bipolarity of relationship that characterizes so much of Western civilization" (Williams 1991, 160). The human subjects who participated in this project did so with the intention of conveying the importance of their bonds with nonhuman animals. It is my goal to employ my research method and writing style to translate these stories into empowerment and acknowledgment. Animals are discarded and animal welfare workers do what they can to maintain a bond between our species. There are times when individuals are sacrificed in order to maintain this bond that our culture, by all obvious accounts, has an inconsistent and terrifying relationship with.

This story is about that tenuous, fragile space between people and the animals most closely bonded with our emotional lives.

The Cultural Construction
of the American Pet

Two researchers who have examined the theoretical implications of study-ing *institutionalized* animal care in great depth are sociologists Arnold Arluke and Clinton Sanders. Prior to examining the social environments of animals and people in shelters, experimental labs, veterinarians' offices, and even Nazi Germany, in *Regarding Animals* (1996), these authors devote two significant chapters to justifying the use of ethnography in studies that involve animals and people. Supporting the premise that ani-mals, like nature, are social constructions, they briefly explore the mean-ing we associate with animals that we bring into our homes. The animals receive names, are associated with a gender (which may include the removal of reproductive organs), are taught the rules through housebreak-ing and training, and are finally thought of as family members. These processes codify an animal and turn it into a "pet." Some researchers sug-gest that pets eternally remain "make believe" family members due to uncontrollable natural processes such as defecation, mating, and even vomiting. Even these "natural" processes can be controlled through spay-ing and behavior modification (Arluke and Sanders 1996, 10–12).

In *Dominance and Affection: The Making of Pets* (1984), Yi Fu Tuan discusses the social practice of pet keeping as a relationship of tenuous sub-mission and control. The process of domesticating animals is itself a story of domination. Animals were bred to be smaller and thus more manage-able. Males were castrated so that breeding could be controlled. The young of any species are more submissive to its superiors, so animals were bred to retain juvenile characteristics. Floppy ears, shortened muzzles, and curly tails are all physical characteristics found only in the puppies of wild counterparts (Tuan 1984, 100–102).

Because dogs were the earliest domesticated species, Tuan suggests that their story offers a valuable perspective on power relation among humans.

> [Dog ownership] exhibits uniquely a set of relationships . . . dominance and affection, love and abuse, cruelty and kindness. . . . The dog calls forth, on the one hand, the best that a human person is capable of—self-sacrificing devotion to a weaker and dependent being, and, on the other hand, the temptation to exercise power in a willful and arbitrary, even perverse, manner. (Tuan 1984, 102)

Though first bred to be useful, dogs were later genetically manipulated for sport and pleasure. As an example, Tuan reminds the reader of the history of a seemingly frivolous and useless dog, the poodle. These dogs were originally bred to be hunters and retrievers. The long thick coats we associate with them came about as a protection against freezing water, and the haircuts which seem so silly to us were developed to free their limbs for swimming while at the same time protecting crucial parts of their body from frigid temperatures. Tuan even offers a practical excuse for tying a ribbon in the dog's tail or topknot—to help the hunter see the animal in the water and through the foliage and underbrush (1984, 104).

Tuan convincingly traces the history of several other breeds to argue that breeding produced not only a docile, manageable pet, but that this docility was brought about by sometimes cruel and ruthless actions. Pekingese are toy dogs that were bred to have flat faces, and this was sometimes accomplished by physically breaking several bones in their noses shortly after birth. I am still surprised that it is necessary to inform people that almost every breed of dog is born with a tail and that they are cut off at young ages to achieve the required aesthetics we associate with boxers, Dobermans, and Australian shepherds. The average person seldom considers these forms of cruelty and abuses such because they are institutionalized, and we might assume veterinarians perform the procedures. When the surgeries are not performed by vets, but are done with a pair of scissors or a rubber band or a razor blade and a rock, peoples caught performing such acts are considered cruel and can be punished under law. It is quite common to intake animals in shelters that have received botched tail docks (performed often by tying rubber bands around the tail until it falls off), ear docks, and even home-performed neuters. I was informed about a case at a shelter in which a dog was found with sev-

Traits associated with great Danes and French poodles. Taken from a mail order catalog, circa 1910–20.

eral rubber bands embedded in his testicles, apparently in an attempt to neuter him. One day I was accepting a box of six-week-old mixed-breed puppies from a gentleman and he proudly informed me that he "went ahead and cut off their tails for ya'." The aesthetic he valued and associated with one half of the puppies' breeding does not typically determine whether or not they are adoptable mutts. In other words, his home tail docking had little to do with their comfort and future, and more to do with his personal taste, and possibly his variety of institutional cruelty.

Tuan's argument is that despite the apparent presence of affection in our relationships with pets, there is also a considerable degree of indifference to their suffering and exploitation of their powerless position. As Tuan quotes, the average time an American keeps a pet is two years. After two years, the animal becomes mature, its behavior, which was so cute as a puppy, is destructive now that it has become large, and it begins to exhibit sexual urges if it has not been neutered (Tuan 1984, 88). Typically animals are brought to shelters from ages six months to two years. This theme of affection, power and control will resurface in the stories the workers tell in following chapters.

Pet keeping, as we know it today, was a middle-class invention of the Victorian era, strongly informed by the class and gender stratification that structured nineteenth-century social life. Author Harriet Ritvo states that pet keeping was not only about love, but was strongly influenced by status and capitalism. People in all socioeconomic classes owned dogs, and their pets became reflections of those class levels (Ritvo 1986, 87, 90). Dog breeding became a middle-class pastime that allowed for the purchase of status, and most of the breeds we are familiar with today were an invention of the Victorian era. Breeding for specific traits became not only focused on the physical appearance of a breed, but on those qualities associated with morality and personality as well. Amateurs approached dog breeding by becoming informed about a breed's moral standing through pet care and compliance. These qualities were associated with breed as opposed to individual, and the amateur breeder probably had little knowledge of the results of breeding animals to produce these "moral" qualities (Kete 1994, 70).

As life became increasingly removed from a rural past, and culture became separated from nature, the animals that lived in nineteenth-century homes become denatured and "civilized." Modifying animal behavior, according to historian Kathleen Kete, entailed the "transformation of beastly behavior into quasi-human conduct" (1994, 77). Pet care books, which were relatively absent from the culture prior to the beginning of the nineteenth century, instructed Parisians on the methods for "civilizing" an animal to make him a more desirable family member. These methods, according to Kete, translated into feminizing, de-animalizing, and denaturing pets (especially dogs) in order to control their "animal" urges. They were fed from the table, dressed in clothes, groomed, housebroken, closely controlled during heat cycles to ensure they would not be contaminated by undesirable (i.e., lower-class) mates, taught tricks for amusement at parties. It was suggested by some authors that pets be euthanized once they reached a certain age to avoid placing undue emotional or physical strain on human family members. Nineteenth-century Parisians viewed pets as eternal children, going so far as to wed them prior to mating and to bury them in elaborate pet cemeteries (1994, 77–94).

Cats also received a similar process of incorporation, but for different reasons than dogs. Dogs were acclaimed because of the notion of fidelity. Kete suggests that fidelity became a highly valued trait in nineteenth-century France because of the alienation and isolation brought about by modern industrial life in urban environments. Pets were kept so that people did not have to die alone, and they were glorified for their steadfast loyalty even beyond the lives of their owners. Newspapers and humane societies published reports of incredible journeys dogs made to be reconciled with owners, dog suicides, and dogs rescuing owners from the Seine. Fidelity was a concept that was classless; dogs were faithful to owners no matter how rich or poor, how kind or cruel (Kete 1994, 22–35). Cats, on the other hand, took longer to incorporate and required a route that neutralized historical associations. Kete describes cats, according to the nineteenth-century worldview, as sexually charged and independent. "This characteriza-tion of the cat as both feminine and sensual was an inheritance from German and Egyptian paganism" (Kete 1994, 119). They were ritually sac-rificed, and were often the victims of more horrifying examples of abuse. It was through bohemia that these animals were gradually accepted as pets, as intellectuals honored them for the very traits that made them difficult to integrate into nineteenth-century middle-class life. "Like the intellectual, the cat held in limbo, so to speak, values forced to the margins of bourgeois life" (Kete 1994, 125). By the end of the nineteenth century, pet keeping had become formulaic and cats were accepted as house pets (Kete 1994, 115–135).

The humane societies, according to these authors, had a profound effect on how animals were incorporated into bourgeois life. This was mainly through the publication of their annual reports, and their desire to involve the average citizen in the crusade to enforce anti-cruelty laws. Ritvo states that the rhetoric of the Society of the Prevention of Cruelty to Animals (later known as the RSPCA after it received royal patronage from Queen Victoria) was as much about social control as it was about "sympathy for its victims" (1986, 133). In this, the humane movement was similar to other crusades. Perpetrators of violence against animals were portrayed with little sympathy in humane society accounts, which were almost always portrayals of lower-class individuals. Ritvo suggests that the RSPCA avoided criticizing upper-class cruelty, such as steeple chasing and fox hunting, and focused their efforts on the moral degeneracy of the poor. I would add that in many cases, the humane societies depended on patronage from the aristocracy, and they chose their battles according to a consciousness of the source of their fund-ing. The rhetoric the RSPCA employed when describing acts of cruelty had a tendency to "isolate and stigmatize" large *poor* sections of the population (Ritvo 1986, 136).

The most horrifying acts of cruelty documented by the societies were committed during the normal course of business affairs. Cart and draft horses were routinely beaten and neglected; animals driven to slaughter were portrayed as being treated with contempt and violence. Crimes against pets, however, held the most attraction in these reports, and were documented with more frequency than crimes against draft animals, despite the fact that these happened more frequently. Ritvo suggests that this is due to the ability of the average citizen to identify with the animal victims in the stories, and that in raising pets to be trustful and friendly to humans, the average Victorian citizen was somehow implicated in these crimes. The narratives found in these reports were formulaic and inevitably predictable, though they varied greatly in length and detail. As Ritvo states, the stories "emphasized both the gratuitousness and the grotesqueness of their sufferings and the corollary moral depravity of their torturers" (1986, 141). Animal victims were described as sympathetically as possible. Their patience, resignation, childlike ignorance, and powerlessness were often emphasized. "The more blameless the victims, the more horrifying the crimes, and the more depraved the perpetrator" (Ritvo 1986, 142–143).

Despite the fact that the lower classes did at times publicly rebel against these laws and continued to attend dog fights and other forms of animal amusements, the RSPCA succeeded in codifying animal abuse as a form of social class deviance.

According to author James Turner in *Reckoning with the Beast: Animals, Pain, and Humanity in the Victorian Mind* (1980), several factors contributed to a growing interest in the humane treatment of animals. Industrialization brought about a romanticized view of rural life and the creatures associated with it. Medical advances, such as the use of anesthetics in the mid- to late nineteenth century, made people more conscious of pain and suffering and more empathetic with suffering in others. The acceptance of a kinship with animals, brought about by a willingness to accept the theories of natural selection and evolution, made people realize that they owed a kindness towards the creatures with whom they shared existence (Turner 1980, 82–83, 127).

> ### How to Treat a Man
> ### By a Horse
>
> WHEN A MAN drops from sheer exhaustion, seize an end-board or cart stake and pound him on the head and ribs. If this does not recuperate him, kick him violently in the stomach. If persistently adhered to, this will restore him. If a man finds his load too heavy and that it will strain him to proceed, kick off a fenceboard, knock him down and hammer him thoroughly. This will give him renewed energy. Do not on any account reduce his load. If a man refuses to drink when you offer him water, do not give him any for two days. That will teach him to be thirsty at your convenience.
>
> It is a good plan to ply the whip frequently. No matter if he is doing his best, hit him now and then on general principles to prevent him from taking any comfort. If his load is not heavy, oblige him to go faster to make up for it. Tie his head back in an unnatural position with eyes toward the sun. This will give him a fine appearance and prevent stumbling. In winter remove his clothing to "prevent his taking cold." He will also dry quicker when you overwork him. Men thus treated are much healthier than when wearing thick coats.
>
> We are indebted for this satire to our friend, J. Hansell French, Secretary of Agriculture for Pennsylvania, who clipped it from Hoard's Dairyman.
>
> ---
>
> WE WERE TOLD that a horse had stood from 10 A. M. to 4 P. M. near Second and Walnut Streets. Though blanketed, that was much too long in zero weather. Our agent found the driver. a Negro, nearby. He explained he had a job to move a load of wood: had been put off from hour to hour; had pawned his overcoat to rent the horse. When paid, he would redeem his coat; have enough left over for his supper. In such a case, said we, just drive round the block at intervals. We wished him luck, were sorry we could not bring the person responsible for the delay before a magistrate.
>
> ---
>
> ONE OF OUR AGENTS uses his Sundays to feed birds at his own expense back in the woods in Delaware County. An old family custom.

A cruelty report taken from *Animaldom*, the annual report of The Pennsylvania Society for the Prevention of Cruelty to Animals, March 1936.

Turner documents the growth of the animal welfare movement in England and America and explains that pet keeping was another way that people developed a kinship with animals. The growth of middle-class pet keeping, in particular, gave these classes of people a sense of humanitarianism that neither threatened their class complacency nor caused undue social unrest. Along with the growth in pet keeping came the increased awareness of suffering among animals. In 1824 in England, the first meeting of the Society for the Prevention of Cruelty to Animals was held. These founders believed it was possible, through education and the enforcement of anti-cruelty laws, to teach the lower classes about the humane treatment of animals. This crusade was not confined to a concern for the animals used for work or sport; it was believed that a sense of kindness would have a ripple effect and lead towards the creation of a gentler society. Advocating a doctrine of stewardship towards animals would lead to a general uplifting of the lower classes, making urban living less threatening and violent. This involved, as Ritvo states it, a need to "redefine the social location of concern for animals" (1986, 129).

These themes were not restricted to the treatment of horses and bulls, although the first laws enacted did specifically focus on these animals. The rise of medical science and scientific authority in Victorian England also brought about a suspicion of the methods doctors and scientists employed to investigate nature. The people most suspicious of those methods were primarily upper- and middle-class women, and the focal point of their distrust centered on the use of vivisection as a methodological tool. Vivisection produced debates over the sanctity of life, freedom from suffering, and the power of science. These debates have been examined in a number of texts, but most notably by Coral Lansbury in *The Old Brown Dog: Women, Workers, and Vivisection in Edwardian England* (1985). The women involved in movements to abolish vivisection were typically also involved in other humanitarian causes, including the abolition of slavery, suffrage, and the settlement movement. Concern for the poor, for children and women, and for animals became intertwined, and the experiences of animals became a point of identification for the women advocating their rights. Although the movement was stronger in England, American women were also appalled by what they considered the cruel effects of classroom vivisection on young people. The first laws to abolish educational vivisection in the public schools were enacted in Massachusetts in 1894 (Buettinger 1997, 862–863). These authors propose that women, either from the elite classes of scientists or doctors, or the working classes and poor, were drawn to these welfare causes because women actually identified with the animals they defended. Lansbury looks at this argument in depth, suggesting that Victorian gynecology and pornography had striking similarities to the experiences of animals, and that *Black Beauty*, published in 1877, could be considered a veiled feminist tract (Lansbury 1985, 129). The ecofeminist idea that oppressions are linked, including oppression of women, people of color, the poor, animals, and nature, is echoed in subtle ways throughout Lansbury's work.

Efforts to form humane societies in the United States followed England by about a half a century. Caroline Earle White, an educated and wealthy activist in Philadelphia, wanted to organize a humane society in the 1850s. Her goal was delayed by the Civil War. It wasn't until 1866 that the first society was formed in the United States. Henry Bergh, a wealthy public figure in New York, returned from travels in Russia and Europe and decided to emulate the formation of the SPCA in England by organizing the American Society for the Prevention of Cruelty to Animals (hereafter ASPCA) in New York City. Although laws had been passed as early as 1828 to protect animals, there was little or no enforcement of these laws. Bergh successfully organized the wealthy and elite of New York City and established the first humane organization in this country (Finsen and Finsen 1994, 42–47; Turner 1980, 45–51). With his encouragement, White organized the PSPCA in Philadelphia only a year after Bergh. Her gender prevented her from having an active role in the leadership of this organization, so in 1869 she formed the Women's Philadelphia Society for the Prevention of Cruelty to Animals (WPSPCA). White proved an effective leader and the wealth present in the organization led to quick reforms. "Barely a month after its founding, the WPSPCA had already persuaded the mayor of Philadelphia to erect more merciful facilities for killing stray dogs; before its second birthday it had its own animal shelter, which had entirely taken over from the city the collection and disposal of strays" (Turner 1980, 51).

By 1922, according to historian William J. Shultz, there were 539 active humane societies registered with the American Humane Association. American Humane formed in 1877 to serve as a national agency responsible for bringing together animal welfare agencies across the country and throughout the world. Because most animal welfare agencies also extended their protective services to include children, American Humane has both a child and an animal welfare division (Shultz 1924, 50).

The more radical issues, such as vivisection, humane slaughter, and vegetarianism were eventually excluded from the mainstream animal welfare movement by the end of the nineteenth century (Finsen and Finsen 1994, 51). Activists concerned with these causes formed their own splinter groups and avoided the conservative complacency of humane organizations. From the early 1900s until about the 1950s, humane societies were mainly responsible for housing stray and unwanted animals and investigating cruelty. Little legislation or drastic changes in policy occurred during this period (Finsen and Finsen 1994, 50–53; Kete 1994, 19; Shultz 1924, 64–65). Kathleen Kete suggests that the focus on stray and homeless animals came about as a retreat from the "dangerous and masculine scientific world" and that instead of resisting the institution of science, many women channeled their efforts towards caring for homeless animals (Finsen and Finsen 1994, 53–54; Turner 1980, 17). Turner explains that while these founding animal welfare groups were led by the upper classes, they appealed and were accessible to the middle classes. "Sensitivity to their basically conservative, middle-class constituency conditioned their every move . . . to have behaved otherwise would have jeopardized the SPCA mission" (Turner 1980, 58). While the movement to protect domestic animals from cruelty and neglect became accepted by the mainstream in both England and America, it proposed no radical changes to the status of animals and reinforced the idea of stewardship. Stewardship involves a paternalistic care for the less powerful members of a society, and is often associated with biblical verses that commanded Adam to be a steward of God's creatures. The founders of the welfare movement in America and England strove towards humane treatment of animals (such as humane slaughter and transportation); they did not advocate the abolition of these practices. So while animals still maintained little rights other than the right not to suffer, this theme, which Turner calls "sympathy for suffering," became a dominant value in Anglo-American culture (1980, 58–59).

Control of Pet Populations

To understand the issues plaguing workers in modern shelters, it makes sense to discuss what is known about how companion animal populations were controlled in our recent past. Kete spends one chapter of her book discussing the efforts of the Parisian government to institute a dog tax in the mid-nineteenth century. It was believed that the large dog population of the country meant that a large human population of the city was starving in order to feed the dogs. Although the tax ultimately failed because of faulty design and implementation, this is one of the first

Billboard encouraging spay/neuter in Willamette Valley, 1989.

instances in these historical works where concern was raised over the number of animals present in urban environments (Kete 1994, 47–54).

Following outbreaks or instances of disease, especially rabies, the populace routinely thinned out the stray-animal populations. Cat populations were also thinned at various times during the year, but typically by mobs for ritual purposes. Kete notes that these ritual murders often accompanied fertility rites and other observances of a religious nature. As recently as 1905, cats were rounded up and placed in a metal cage to be burned in observance of festivals and saint's days (Kete 1994, 119). These rituals were observed in accordance with the cats' association with paganism and sexuality.

Companion animal medicine was also a relatively late development in Europe and America. Prior to the nineteenth century, blacksmiths treated sick and injured animals, since veterinary science was not institutionalized until the 1800s. Most of these early vets were concerned with treating horses and cattle and other forms of livestock. Dog and cat medical care remained primarily a responsibility of the family (Kete 1994, 78–79).

Understanding the pathology of rabies, distemper, and other contagious diseases had to wait until advances were made in microbiology, parasitology, and immunology. These fields were slow to apply this knowledge to the treatment of canine and feline diseases, leaving few effective weapons against these diseases until after World War II (Dunlop and Williams 1996, 601). Distemper was easily considered one of the most devastating contagious illnesses among animal populations, often causing enough extermination of livestock animals to cripple the economic affairs of affected regions (Dunlop and Williams 1996, 603). An effective vaccine against the disease was not developed until 1928 (Dunlop and Williams 1996, 607). Cats were not immune to epidemics, despite their relatively antisocial lifestyles. Panleukopenia, a dreaded cat plague, was also not understood until as late as 1928. This disease is closely related to a later developing virus that effects canine populations, called parvovirus, which did not appear as a national epidemic until 1977 (Dunlop and Williams 1996, 615–616). While great advances have been made in the last sixty years to combat these illnesses, they continue to affect animal populations and require vaccines to keep them controlled.

They do not, it appears, have sufficient power to keep the pet population in balance. Although current statistics vary widely according to the source, national welfare groups suggest that 4–6 million pets are killed in animal shelters and control facilities every year in the United States. Neuters and spays have been performed on animals since the beginnings of domestication in order to control breeding populations. They were performed without anesthesia prior to the twentieth century. Kete includes documentation in her work that estimated that one in fifteen cats in Paris were neutered in the mid-nineteenth century (1994, 122). With the rise of the use of anesthesia in surgery in the late nineteenth and early twentieth centuries, spaying and neutering has become a routine and safe practice in veterinary clinics and animal shelters. In the early part of the twentieth century, many larger, well-funded humane societies opened animal hospitals in conjunction with their shelters (Shultz 1924, 75).

The humane societies of the nineteenth and twentieth centuries had long been concerned with the humane disposal of surplus animals in urban environments. "In New York City, for instance, prior to 1894 the old city dog pound was a place of horror. Dogs were destroyed by drowning, and by the supplementary use of clubs in case of escape from water" (McCrea 1910, 86–89). Animals who could not be placed in new homes were killed in gas chambers. Over 108,000 animals were killed in these chambers in New York in 1907 (1910, 88). It was the goal of many humane societies at the turn of the century to provide quick and painless deaths for surplus animals, and the best method at the time was with the use of gas chambers.

William J. Shultz, whose 1924 history of the movement followed Roswell McCrea's, quotes from a Boston animal protection policy book regarding the disposal of surplus animals. The League states that they would keep all dogs, unless sick or vicious, for five days, and that they would choose twenty to thirty of the "best" cats and kittens. The rest were "put to death" (Shultz 1924, 65). The policy statement continued by explaining that their goal was to "prevent and to release animals from suffering," and therefore they did not "keep a large number of animals alive" (Shultz 1924, 66). Keeping them from starving on the street was simply not enough—humane societies also turned their attention to how the animals were treated in pounds and shelters. Shultz notes that although many humane societies were founded with the sole purpose of performing cruelty investigations, such as the Kentucky Humane Society in Louisville, Kentucky, they were often enlisted to alter inhumane practices at city pounds. When these organizations either refused to take over pounds, or could not due to internal conflicts, others formed to perform those relief services (Shultz 1924, 68). Typically, prior to the involvement of humane societies, dogs and cats in city pounds were drowned, shot or hung (Kete 1994, 19–20), if they weren't first abused by dog pound officials or utilized by other perpetrators of animal cruelty—the vivisectionists. Pound seizure remains a source of criticism for city pounds and humane societies in the United States. Shelter workers have long battled to provide a safe haven for stray animals, while scientists have attempted to utilize this surplus population for their own purposes. As Finsen and Finsen explain, some states have laws that require shelters and pounds to turn animals over to researchers if they request them.

Professional breeders, especially rural breeders, did not hesitate to control the populations of their litters by employing a culling technique and to only allow desirable offspring to survive or breed. The practice of culling and selective breeding may have become less frequent as populations became more urban, removed from the realities of animal reproduction. In keeping with the incorporation of pets into families, amateur breeders may have become less likely to commit the "crime" of murdering the offspring of personal pets. I would like to suggest that the humane society as a cultural force has had a serious influence on the application of this concept, removing culling from the realm of the average citizen and placing it within an institutional context—not of the veterinarian, but of the euthanasia technician. A friend who worked for a brief period at a humane society in Tucson, Arizona, reported to me that a local great Dane breeder would periodically make a "donation" of entire litters of pups. These pups would have to be immediately euthanized by the humane society workers because of the hip dysplasia that was evident even during the first few months of their lives (Beard, personal communication). The breeder not only was avoiding the culling of her own litters; by turning them in to a humane society she avoided the high fees a veterinarian would charge to perform a service, as well as the likelihood that a veterinarian would report her bloodline to the American Kennel Club.

In keeping with the idea that cruelty to animals is a form of social degeneracy, modern humane societies have removed the killing of animals from the experience of the average citizen. They have also created a rhetoric that suggests that the "backyard" breeding of pet animals is a form of cruelty and neglect, typically committed only by those less educated, callous, greedy, or poorer members of our society. One of the more controversial and successful attempts to lower the euthanasia rate in the United States occurred in San Mateo County, California, in the late 1980s. Activists and welfarists successfully passed legislation that placed a six-month moratorium on breeding in that county to measure its effect on the animal population. Workers at the Peninsula Humane Society in San Mateo County televised euthanasias in order to dramatize the killing that resulted from a saturated breeding community. The efforts unfortunately resulted in little more than a required license for breeding, an ordinance that many urban areas have, but few enforce. While humane societies may go to some extremes to get across the severity of the problem they face, they still often rely on class and gender to formulate their rhetoric, and repeatedly represent animals as powerless, voiceless victims of moral depravity.

> If animal suffering was caused by people in need of moral uplift, then to work for the protection of the brute creation was simultaneously to promote the salvation of human souls and the maintenance of social order. (Ritvo 1986, 132)

In the 1950s there was some legislation passed regarding the humane treatment of food animals and wild horses and burros, but the cultural power of technology following World War II allowed for little criticism of the new techniques of factory farming or animal research. Although groups such as the Humane Society of the United States (HSUS) were founded in reaction to the complacency of welfare organizations such as the American Humane Association (AHA), it wasn't until the 1960s and 1970s—in conjunction with other civil rights activism—that these issues would once again receive public attention (Finsen and Finsen 1994, 54–57). Laws such as the Metcalfe-Hatch Act, which required New York pounds to release animals to researchers, were challenged by humane groups, average citizens, and politicians in the 1960s following highly publicized cases of animal theft and institutional cruelty. Publications such as Peter Singer's *Animal Liberation* (1975) gave the animal rights movement a philosophy and a method to organize around. While many humane societies continued to concern themselves only with the care of stray and unwanted pets, other groups were making their voices heard on national, politicized issues (Finsen and Finsen 1994, 56–71). Animal activists Ingrid Newkirk and Alex Pacheco formed the most recognizable of the radical groups in 1980. People for the Ethical Treatment of Animals, or PETA, continues to produce strong feelings and controversy and is easily one of the most recognizable animal rights organizations in the world. Thanks to high visibility, PETA's activists have managed to increase public awareness of many animal rights issues (Finsen and Finsen 1994, 76–84).

William Shultz states that as humane societies became increasingly more organized in the first two decades of the twentieth century, they became less preoccupied with punishment and more involved with prevention. He quotes an SPCA manager as stating,

> It has taken nearly a half-century of waging warfare upon the cruelist [sic] to break down his indifference to the rights of lower creatures by the law enforcement. It is, therefore, only in recent years that organized humane forces have undertaken another line of attack through constructive methods to make certain his defeat. The punishment of the wrong-doer is not so important in this day as the application of a remedy to cure him of his shortcomings. (Shultz 1924, 99)

Prevention of pet overpopulation was the one issue that brought more radical splinter groups back in solidarity with conservative humane groups (Finsen and Finsen 1994, 150). As authors Rowan and Williams document, a series of articles in the early 1970s brought this issue to public attention. The Humane Society of the United States, under the supervision of Phyllis Wright, started a program aimed at confronting pet overpopulation. Called the "LES" program (legislation, education, and sterilization), this plan led to the establishment of low-cost veterinary clinics in urban areas, classroom education aimed at teaching the importance of sterilization, the advent of early-age spay/neuters, and the requirement that any animal adopted from a shelter be sterilized. Shelters and pounds reported to HSUS that by the 1980s, the number of animals they handled had decreased dramatically (Rowan and Williams 1997, 110–111). In addition, the animals handled by pounds and shelters seem to have changed demographically from unwanted litters to young, untrained dogs and cats (Patronek 1996, 1). Despite visible decreases, the problem of pet overpopulation still appears to be an issue. Humane societies cannot be led into the belief that aggressive spay/neuter programs are enough to control overpopulation. As Rowan and Williams suggest, and I concur, these programs must be integrated with adequate animal control and education programs (1997, 120). Unfortunately, as even the history of Albuquerque's welfare community will illustrate, reliable assistance from municipal pounds is an unusual occurrence.

Finsen and Finsen explain that although modern animal rights activists have been more focused on institutional forms of animal abuse, such as research and farming, the issue of pet overpopulation is one that welfarists and activists agree must be controlled. By the late 1980s, shelters and pounds began to openly express their disgust over handling such large numbers of animals, a great percentage of which were destroyed due to a lack of homes. The rhetoric humane societies had relied upon for a century seemed to have no real effect on significantly lowering the pet population. Spay/neuter programs and education programs did not reach the people who were determined to continue breeding animals for a profit. Many researchers lament the inability to reach accurate statistics regarding the pet population in this country. Andrew N. Rowan states even a 5 percent euthanasia rate should not be acceptable (1997, 142). Whether the figure is six million, as HSUS claims, or two million, as sociologist Gary Patronek and others suggest, this activity remains a dysfunctional system of handling supposedly cherished animal companions (1996, 572).

Despite efforts to collaborate, there is still some dissension among activists who were dissatisfied with what they perceived as the continued complacency of welfarists in traditional shelters. Tom Regan, in *The Case for Animal Rights*, very carefully delineated the philosophical reasons why "euthanasia" is an improper term to apply to the deaths of animals in shelters (1983, 109–116). Euthanasia implies a merciful death, which comes about to relieve suffering, and yet numerous animals are destroyed based merely on a lack of space, or *the potential* for suffering. Gary Francione particularly criticizes the position of welfarists, who he believes claim that an end to animal suffering can come about through gradual means of changing public opinions towards animals. In *Rain without Thunder: The Ideology of the Animal Rights Movement* (1996), Francione states that the only method that will efficiently end animal suffering is the complete abolition of their use.

These arguments, in my opinion, unfairly set up an opposition between groups that ideologically claim the same goals. In addition, instead of creating an atmosphere of cooperation, they place the welfarists in a position of having to defend themselves against other animal activists, in addition to altering the habits of the general public. One well-known animal activist does not view animal welfare work in such a negative light, partly because she performed welfare work in the 1970s. In September 1991, Ingrid Newkirk, the current president of People for the Ethical

Treatment of Animals (PETA), addressed an audience of animal activists with a paper titled "Dark Angels and Direct Action." In the paper, she gently criticizes those members of the activist cause who seek to distance themselves from the necessary and "dirty work" that takes place in animal shelters and city pounds. She also reminds her audience that the first humane societies, the ASPCA in New York and the Massachusetts SPCA, were founded by men who were keenly interested in the rights of animals, but did not seek to abolish their interdependence with people.

She continues by criticizing those who believe that any home is better than death. Her statement supports the idea that a quality life is far better than a lengthy, painful life—an argument we will return to in later chapters. She also states, "Opening no-kill shelters is not a solution, any more than is taking two or ten animals into one's own home" (Newkirk 1991, 5). She recognizes that no-kill groups can only handle a small number of animals, while the rest continue to be sent to animal control facilities and traditional shelters.

While pet overpopulation is a problem these many disparate groups can agree needs to be solved, how to do so remains a source of contention. The growing division between groups that endorse euthanasia as a method of population control and those that do not has been a primary issue within animal welfare for the past decade. Increasingly, the individuals who believe euthanasia is ineffective are mobilizing and drawing financial support for their efforts. The current popularity and success of companion animal sanctuaries such as Best Friends, a ranch in Kanab, Utah, which houses no fewer than 1,800 animals at a time, is evidence that there remains an uncomfortable lack of effective responses to pet population control.

We will later return to this conflict as it plays out on a local level in one animal welfare community. In summary, animal welfare, since its inception, has encompassed a wide variety of approaches, philosophies, and methods. It involves an active (re)construction of the concept of the human-animal relationship. Now we will see how a very different but similarly oriented group of people grew into a multifaceted and complex welfare community.

3

Animal Welfare in Albuquerque, 1947–Present

In one of the closets at the animal shelter, I was shown a marvelous treasure, one that a researcher almost never finds. Boxes filled with scrapbooks, photographs, newspaper clippings, minutes from meetings, and old newsletters had been piled up and virtually ignored since the collection had begun in the late 1960s. The materials were not in the best shape, but thankfully a dry climate prevented them from decaying sooner. I also found remnants of some anonymous person's collection of dog care and breed books, annual conference booklets, and humane society annual reports from early in the twentieth century.

In addition, I was introduced to a person who was a living resource for almost forty years of history. Thelma Evans was happy to answer any questions I had about the history of Albuquerque's animal welfare community. Her role cannot be ignored in this history. She and her husband were responsible for the growth and success of Albuquerque's largest non-profit private shelter, the Animal Humane Association of New Mexico, Inc. (AHANM or AHA). Although Colonel Evans died in 1988, the legacy he left to the animal welfare community is still felt.

Thelma also provided me with several scrapbooks to trace historical details. A woman by the name of Marianne Newton clipped animal-related articles from the *Albuquerque Tribune* and the *Albuquerque Journal* from the time she moved to Albuquerque in 1951 from Vincennes, Indiana. Page after page reveals the brief stories of shelter animals seeking homes (Pet of the Week), stories of neglect and cruelty, the goings on of the various agencies, the efforts of average citizens, the dramatic politics between and within agencies, but most importantly the success of the animal welfare community in this southwestern city. Members of the organizations provided additional data for this section. I must thank these storytellers and memory keepers for contributing to this project. It is from these sources—newspaper articles, meeting minutes, newsletters, and interviews with Thelma—that I have drawn the following historical sketch.

In April 1947, a meeting was called in Albuquerque, New Mexico, to discuss the formation of a new group of citizens concerned with the welfare of companion animals. Led by T. H. Prather, who was elected chairman of the newly formed group, a plan was drafted to take over the existing dog pound. As it had happened in several other cities across the country, so it began in Albuquerque. Local citizens, dissatisfied with conditions in poorly managed, loosely constructed county pounds, organized to instill a sense of compassion and caring towards the animals in their urban environments. Prior to the twentieth century, as I have mentioned, the concentration of citizens in urban areas was smaller and disease was more likely to keep animal populations in control. As Americans became increasingly urbanized and suburbanized in the twentieth century, and as pet keeping became more associated with middle-class prosperity, the need to control the population became more pressing. In May 1947, papers were drawn for incorporation of the first private organization in New Mexico concerned with the welfare of animals. Calling themselves the Humane Association for the Prevention of Cruelty to Animals of Bernalillo County (shortened later to Bernalillo County Humane Association), the group first listed a series of grievances against the dog pound and stated their interest in taking over care of the city's stray animal population and cruelty investigations. Among those who criticized the pound were members of the newly formed group and a veterinarian named Dr. Glen Bolton.

Failure to provide running water, provide a humane death (done at this time by means of lethal decompression), adequately notify owners if their dogs were impounded, and properly house the animals with consideration of health and quarantine were among the complaints the Association and Dr. Bolton listed against the dog pound. In addition, there were no set fees for claiming or adopting animals, nowhere to house cats, and inspections of the facility were described as infrequent and "haphazard." The Association planned to recruit 2,000 members, thereby creating enough revenue through membership fees to set their plan into motion (*Albuquerque Journal*, 12 July 1947).

As soon as the group formed they were inundated with problems, both internal and external. They established an office downtown for a pet listing service, providing potential pet owners with a place to call to adopt a pet. Instead they received more calls than they could handle from people needing to place unwanted pets. Dog poisonings in Albuquerque seemed rampant, due in large part to the lack of a Poison Control Act in the state of New Mexico and the ability of animals to roam freely with little enforcement of containment laws. When elected officials of the Association began meeting with

---

HELP

THE HUMANE ASSOCIATION BUILD A SHELTER FOR HOMELESS ANIMALS!

TAG DAY—SATURDAY, NOVEMBER 15

—MEMBERSHIP DRIVE WEEK—

NOVEMBER 15 THRU NOVEMBER 22

VOLUNTEER WORKERS—Urgently needed to assist in this humane work. If you are a lover of pets or animals, help by contacting Humane Office, 302½ West Central, Phone 3-5321.

This Space Courtesy of the

PUBLIC SERVICE CO. OF NEW MEXICO

Albuquerque Tribune and Journal, 14 November 1947.

A clipping advertising "Tag Day," which licensed city dogs and raised funds for the new animal shelter.

---

city officials in order to lease city land for the erection of a new facility, other members of the Association opposed mingling with the city for funding and resources (*Albuquerque Tribune*, 17 March 1948).

Funding was the main problem the Association encountered immediately. Although "Tag Days" were held in an effort to encourage Albuquerque citizens to license their pets, there was little enforcement of this city ordinance. The newly elected president, Mrs. Alice M. Woolston, approached city officials and proposed a plan to match a $5,000 award of money with donations to build a new shelter (*Albuquerque Journal*, 24 December 1947). Her plan was to become the site of turmoil within the organization, resulting in city involvement. The opposing members believed that if the city were allowed to become involved in the efforts of a private group, they would eventually oust the group from the management of the shelter. In the early part of 1948, the Association appeared in court to settle these conflicts. Mrs. Marguerite Morgan, the critic, asserted that a shelter could be built for less than $10,000, and all that it would need would be twenty dog runs, a lethal chamber, and a room for the preparation of food. Mrs. Woolston, Morgan claimed, was seeking funding for a hospital and clinic as well.

Alice Woolston filed a suit against those members of the Humane Association who were holding the shelter construction in question. The suit was resolved and it favored the plan to collaborate with the city. In April 1948, despite the criticisms of Morgan, who believed that the new shelter would eventually become nothing more than a "dog pound," the

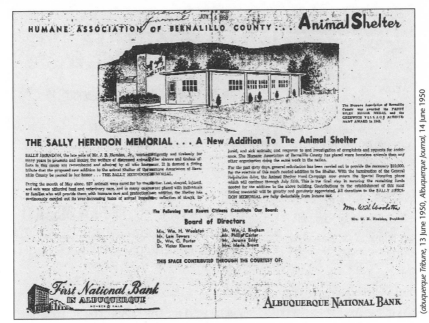

(abuquerque Tribune, 13 June 1950, Albuquerque Journal, 14 June 1950)

The Bernalillo County Animal shelter in the early 1950s.

city agreed to match funds for this project. In early 1949, the $10,000 shelter was erected at Las Lomas and Wyoming. An addition was added in the early 1950s.

The Bernalillo County Animal Shelter managed to obtain a truck for animal pickups and immediately found themselves in financial straits again due to the low compliance of the purchase of city licenses. Once again the city was asked to assist in the effort to enforce this ordinance. Recruitment of local police and publicity of the new law caused the population to purchase licenses faster than they could be supplied. In only two days in August, 184 licenses were issued to dog owners. The Association also apparently raised funds with membership drives, with a one-year membership cost of $5.00 (source for information from a membership card found in the scrapbook for a Ruth L. Owens, 1 June 1951).

Animals adopted from the shelter were vaccinated against distemper (at this time rabies inoculations were not yet required by law) and females were spayed. The shelter administrators pleaded with the citizens of Albuquerque to discontinue dumping animals, asking that they be called to come pick them up instead. Under the supervision of Mrs. Woolston, the shelter began to grow and have an effect on the community. It was noted that the number of dog bites decreased and animals were humanely disposed of by the shelter. In February 1952, the paper adver-

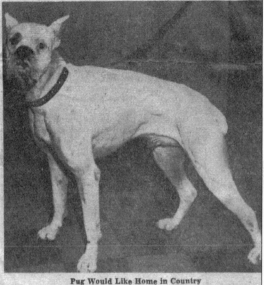

Deaf Boxer Is Pet of the Week; He Needs a Home in Country

A deaf white Boxer is The Tribune's pet of the week today.

His name is Pug. He was mentioned in a Tribune story last month when he was at the Albuquerque Animal Shelter. Someone read the article and gave him home.

But at that time it wasn't known that he is deaf. The man who adopted Pug had to return him to the shelter after learning of the handicap because Pug's new home was in an area of busy streets. Since the dog hears nothing, the man was afraid he would get hit by a car.

So Pug again needs a master. V. A. Rouse, shelter manager, wants to find the two year old a place to live in the country where he will have plenty of room to run and play without so much chance of getting hurt because of his deafness.

The dog is healthy and is fond of children, Mr. Rouse said, and would make a rural resident a good pet.

Anyone interested in adopting Pug can see him at the shelter between 1 and 5 any day except Friday or Saturday. The shelter gives no information about pets over the phone.

Pug Would Like Home in Country

Albuquerque Tribune, 12 March 1956

An early "Pet of the Week" advertisement.

tised that thirty-five dogs were available for adoption at the shelter, and the article listed some of the policies the shelter enforced that guaranteed that these dogs would receive good homes. Big dogs were only adopted out to people who lived in the country, and no family with children under six was permitted to adopt puppies and kittens.

In January 1953, the *Albuquerque Tribune* ran the first "Pet of the Week" article. These weekly postings became a successful vehicle for placing animals, and continue to be so to the present day. Originally, the ads focused on purebred dogs, such as a great Dane, a dalmatian, a then rare breed called a basenji, and several cocker spaniels. They offer an excellent history of the popularity of breeds and breed mixes, stories of cruelty and neglect, and they were almost always followed up, providing readers with stories of their successful adoptions. One of these was the adoption of a poorly presented little dachshund by Marianne Newton.

In 1956 the shelter manager, V. A. Rouse, reported that the city shelter handled 10,000 pets. That year, the County Animal Protective Society merged with the Association to make a "stronger and more efficient unit"

(*Albuquerque Tribune*, 22 February 1956). City ordinances passed during this time exerted more control over the keeping of pets in the city, requiring that animals held at the shelter be destroyed if not claimed or adopted after five days. There was also an attempt to pass a law requiring rabies vaccinations (*Albuquerque Tribune*, 22 February; 7 March 1956).

The requirements (including that female dogs be spayed before release) put into effect by the Association came under fire from local veterinarians and citizens. It was believed that these requirements led to the unnecessary high fees for adoption and therefore the deaths of adoptable animals. After a fair amount of pressure was exerted from the Veterinary Association, several changes were instituted at the shelter under city management. The shelter was required to provide a list of all veterinarians in Albuquerque that could offer services such as spay and shots for dogs instead of relying on low-cost veterinary services provided by one or two veterinarians in the city. They were required to send injured animals to these vets, appointed by the Association, prior to admitting them to the shelter. Veterinarians were required to vaccinate the dogs in the shelter, and would be provided for one hour a day during the workweek to do so. The length of time to hold animals before they were euthanized was shortened to only five days (*Albuquerque Tribune*, 11 May 1957).

Letters were written from local citizens that voiced dramatic divisions in opinions of the shelter. F. Grace Nelson wrote a letter to the editor stating her belief that the city shelter was nothing more than a "slaughterhouse" for animals. The *Tribune* responded to her letter by defending the efforts of the "humanitarians" who worked for the shelter, and instead placing the blame on the owners who abandoned their pets. Interestingly, none of the letters found in this collection concerning this debate point specifically to pet overpopulation as the root problem. In most cases, it was believed that irresponsible owners are not those who allow their animals to breed, but those who abandon them or otherwise mistreat them. Pet overpopulation was not directly blamed for high euthanasia rates.

There was, unfortunately, a tragic end to this conflict. After several years of service, V. A. Rouse was required to face eleven counts of mismanagement and irresponsible administration of the shelter (*Albuquerque Tribune*, 11 May 1957). The charges originated in an innocuous oversight; an adopter was charged for the spay and shots of a female dog who had already been adopted from the shelter once before. The irate adopter, rather than seeing Rouse regarding the fee, went to the city commission and filed a complaint. An investigation followed this incident, which initially resulted in the appointment of a management consultant who would assist Rouse in auditing books and improving shelter operations.

Unfortunately, the turmoil present in the Humane Association during these months resulted in Rouse's removal from his position. Since the city had merged with the Humane Association the previous year, the Association had served only as an advisory board and fundraising branch of the shelter. During the investigation, the Association was divided on whether or not to continue backing Rouse as shelter manager. Woolston believed Rouse had done an admirable job and continued lending him her support, despite the city's investigation. "Disagreement over Rouse's operation of the animal shelter is the main bone of contention in association ranks" (*Albuquerque Tribune*, 4 April 1957). In a meeting in May, she was "ousted" from her position as President of the Humane Association, and the vice-president, Mrs. O. Eichelberger, took on that post. The city made a decision to disentangle the shelter from the tumultuous Humane Association, a decision Woolston supported.

Finally, the city decided to remove Rouse from his position despite the concern over his failing health. Rouse was accused of willfully disregarding the legal time limit set to hold animals, of practicing veterinary medicine without a license, of doubling charges for spays and shots, of conducting personal business on city time, of mismanaging financial records and records of animals, and of employing his daughter as his assistant director. He was also accused of failing to inform customers that they could have their new pets inoculated and spayed at any area vet's office, and of being rude to patrons of the shelter. Employees testified that they had been required to work irregular hours (because he and his daughter did), and that they had been asked to do such tasks as hang out clothes and take his granddaughter to school while on city time (*Albuquerque Tribune*, 11, 13, and 17 May 1957).

Rouse was defended by some, including Alice Woolston, but in the end he was held responsible for his mistakes. During Rouse's appeals to the city commission, Mrs. Woolston's husband, a prominent Albuquerque physician, died from heart trouble, undoubtedly removing her from the conflict for an extended period of time. Though Rouse was offered the choice of a demotion, he chose to resign from his position. He claimed that he had hired his daughter after her mother died in a car accident because the shelter was a "husband-wife" run organization, and that the city never fully took responsibility for the shelter's affairs after the takeover. His lawyer asserted, "Because of politics and criticisms from the Humane

Association and veterinarians, the shelter is a hot potato . . . which the city has sidestepped, and for which Mr. Rouse is now the sacrificial lamb." Rouse was finally dismissed on May 10, 1957.

Despite the fact that without her efforts a shelter would have never been built, Woolston's critics seemed to have been on target with the potential dangers of working with the city. The city shelter, still located at Lomas and Wyoming (with additional facilities on the west side of Albuquerque), continues to figure prominently in the development of splinter humane organizations and the rhetoric involving the acceptable treatment of animals. Most of the rescue and welfare groups that have developed in the city of Albuquerque provide animals with an alternative to the "pound," where an adoptable dog or cat might get four to ten days to find a new home. It appears that every decade or so, the city shelter is consistently investigated by humane groups or concerned citizens for charges of cruelty and neglect, mismanagement, and employee theft. Once, employees were even charged with growing marijuana plants on the premises and holding gambling and drinking parties after hours (*Albuquerque Tribune*, 15 January; 24 April; 9 July 1965; *Albuquerque Tribune*, 11 and 13 July 1979; *Humane Society of the United States Report*, 6 June 2000). Since the 1950s, the city animal shelter has increased its shelter animal population from 10,000 a year to 30,000 a year. The ratio of animals adopted to those euthanized remains about the same. In 1967, 17,000 animals were impounded and 12,000 were destroyed. In 1965, a $3,000 decompression chamber was installed that allowed workers to euthanize a number of animals at a time. Currently, the accepted method of euthanasia at the city pound is an injection of sodium pentobarbital.

The responsibility for this pet overpopulation was being blamed on the public by the mid-1960s. In January 1967, the administrator of the pound, Colonel Eugene V. Hughey, stated that the pound was not responsible for destroying pets, the owners who allowed them to breed were (*Heights News*, 26 January 1967). This rhetoric was different from the statements made by past administrators and representatives from humane groups, who credited high shelter populations to owner neglect, abandonment, and disregard for leash laws. The topic of overpopulation and birth control was a situated, contextual event, as far as the Albuquerque humane movement was concerned. As the author of the article even stated, overpopulation and birth control were "current issues" in general, not only as applied to pets (*Heights News*, 26 January 1967). The article went on to discuss the most reliable methods of birth control for pets, quoting a local veterinarian who advocated the penning of females in season. The author only briefly mentioned sterilization, and did so in a manner to imply that this was the last alternative for the overly licentious pet.

The discussion of animal population control was made accessible by the events that were occurring in American culture at that time. The birth control pill became available to women in the mid-1960s, and allowed for a cultural dialogue and an approach to sexuality and reproduction that were more confrontational than in the past. This more relaxed rhetoric about sexuality also allowed for animal welfare workers to confront the public over pet reproduction, and allowed them to blame individual pet owners for a lack of responsibility and control. Responsibility over reproductive freedom extending from the personal freedoms of the individual was applied to the pet population problem in the 1960s and 1970s.

There are currently well over a hundred animal agencies in the state of New Mexico that deal with animal welfare. These include rescue and welfare groups, breed rescue groups and individuals, wildlife rescue groups, endangered species advocacy groups, investigative and rights advocacy groups, and established, traditional shelters. Each varies slightly in approach and orientation, but nearly every group advocates the relief of suffering of animals. At this time I would like to provide some background information on several other groups that arose in Albuquerque in the last four decades. I have interviewed members from three of the groups that deal only with companion animals. These individuals introduce three different methods of dealing with animal rescue and sheltering work, allowing for such variables as volunteerism, employment, various opinions towards euthanasia, fund-raising, and degrees of cooperation with other groups. I will also offer a very brief historical sketch of each organization.

The Tax-Payers' Anti-Cruelty Federation of New Mexico, Inc./The Animal Humane Association of New Mexico, Inc.

In 1965 the Taxpayers' Anti-Cruelty Federation was founded in Albuquerque by a small group of women. The main goal of this organization was to undertake cruelty investigations and provide a lost and found service for stray animals. The group was small (originally three people) and operated out of members' homes (Evans 1999). The founders, including Jean Cowan, were not "little old ladies in tennis shoes," but young housewives intent upon enforcing animal cruelty statutes and returning lost pets to their rightful owners. By 1967 the organization had fifty members and made at least thirty cruelty investigations every month (*Albuquerque Tribune*, 4 June 1966; 1 July 1967).

In the late 1950s, Colonel Edmund Evans and his wife, Thelma, moved to Albuquerque. The Colonel had retired from a career in the Air Force and was working on a degree from the University of New Mexico. Thelma had plans to retire. They brought with them two Yorkshire terriers, a relatively rare breed in this area of the country at that time. Shortly after they arrived, their veterinarian called them and asked if they would be willing to foster a Yorkshire terrier for a group called the Taxpayers' Anti-Cruelty Federation (Evans 1999).

Strays apparently had little hope on the streets of Albuquerque in the early 1960s. According to Thelma, you could find them everywhere. At parties, children would be given puppies as prizes. There were always people in front of stores with sick puppies in boxes to be given away for free. Dead dogs and cats were often seen on the side of the road after being struck by cars. What was even worse, people would dump unwanted animals in "the country," which at that time started at the intersection of Las Lomas and Wyoming, close to the dog pound (Evans 1999).

Eventually the office for the Anti-Cruelty Federation was relocated to the Evanses' home, and the Colonel was elected president of the organization. According to a Federation newsletter from July 1967, the shelter had to stop accepting animals due to lack of resources, and the Federation's animals were boarded at the kennel of a local veterinarian whose family had long been involved with animal welfare issues in Albuquerque (Evans 1999). Adoption clinics were held on Sundays at the boarding kennel. The group managed to place 124 animals in new homes in 1967 (*East Heights News*, 21 March 1968).

In 1968 several changes were made to this organization. First of all, it was decided that a shelter would be built to support the animals they found in the community. In June of that year, the group voted to change its name to the Animal Humane Association of New Mexico, Inc. (AHANM), in order to reflect their "aims and activities." An auxiliary branch of the group was organized by female members, who began conducting garage and yard sales to raise funds for the shelter, with the long-range goal of establishing a thrift shop.

The following spring, the Association announced that it had located land on which to build a shelter. In June 1969, they closed on the property at 615 Virginia, immediately north of Kirtland Air Force Base. The property had

Photo courtesy of AHANM

A photograph of the new kennel at AHA, 615 Virginia, 1970.

a preexisting building that would be used for administrative offices, a cat adoption room, surgery, and receiving animals. In January 1970, plans were made to build a dog kennel. Ed and Thelma were the motivators behind this effort to establish a shelter to be an alternative to the animal control facility. When the property was established at Virginia, they lost members of the group due to their decision to euthanize animals if homes could not be found for them. Some of these individuals—including Jean Hall, a primary member of the Taxpayers' Anti-Cruelty Federation—publicly voiced their concerns over the "new" policies at AHANM. In March 1970, the Evanses were forced to respond to several criticisms made of the organization—including accusations that they were selling purebred animals instead of returning them to their owners, overcharging for claim fees, discriminating against cats, and otherwise mismanaging complaints and requests from the community. They were criticized for asking for donations from people who brought in dogs, only to charge a fee to those who claimed or adopted them. The criticisms made in the newspaper article sound as naive and unreasonable as any criticism from a well-intentioned but otherwise uneducated person who cares for animals. I have many times received criticisms similar to these—the same criticisms thirty years later. Some people do not understand that money must be solicited from the public to care for animals, and that many times original owners are not willing to go to the trouble of paying for shots or driving any distance to pick up their dogs. The Evanses defended the choices they made and attempted to justify their position in an article in the *Albuquerque Journal* on March 15, 1970. They discussed these same concerns with their own members by publishing a newsletter devoted to these criticisms (April 1970).

One of the other critics included the veterinarian who originally worked with Thelma and Ed. Although Thelma and this veterinarian later reconciled to some degree, the division over the group's decision to euthanize kept them at odds for several years. Thelma attributes this to several factors, including the fact that after they built their own shelter, this veterinarian lost a valuable boarding client in the group. More importantly, the moral conflict over euthanasia kept them apart. Thelma explained that the veterinarian asked them to give her any animals that could not be placed.

> They had little spirits and she didn't believe in putting them down. Now they may have little spirits, I won't argue that point. But there's a time when it's the right thing to do, it's not easy to do. . . . Of course at that time they [the pound] used the decompression chamber. Now everybody said that was horrible, but you know I sat there and watched it. I loaded it and unloaded it. And it was not horrible. I think it was easier on the people that had to do it and the animals didn't know what was happening. They were put in a cage and they were nervous, but it was so quick. (Evans 1999)

Years later, when one worker grew frustrated at watching animals she had cared for be mishandled by city workers at the pound, the Association started euthanizing animals by injection on their own premises (Evans 1999). Euthanasia is still the source of a great deal of criticism from the community, from other welfare groups, and even from some of the volunteers who work at AHANM. Thelma responds to what motivated her to get involved and how she managed to justify the decision to euthanize animals in the following statement:

> I think the hardest thing in the world was for me to actually do what I knew needed to be done. For years, in my dreams, I would see a certain set of little eyes that would look at you at the last moment. I know people thought I was very hard and . . . didn't give a damn, but that's a cover-up that I've used since I was a kid because I was always terribly shy and withdrawn. Everything just kind of pushed me back. But I think the thing that really got me interested was we were four years in London and talk about humane groups, you take the English, they know what they're doing and they do it. There isn't anything that they don't take a hand in and see that it's done right. Then to

come back here and see all these boxes of puppies, no shots are given . . . in the box they might have these runny nose and runny eyes. It was horrible, the shock of it I think. (Evans 1999)

AHANM, under the direction of Ed and Thelma Evans, established itself as one of the leading animal welfare agencies in New Mexico over the course of the next thirty years. In 1966, the Anti-cruelty Federation had 11 members and an income of $125.00. By 1969 the membership was up to 781. In 1978, the first full-time kennel worker was hired. The organization since has grown from one run almost entirely by volunteers into a shelter that employs approximately forty full-time workers and has a volunteer base of over four hundred people. Ed and Thelma worked ten- to twelve-hour days caring for strays and owner-surrendered pets. They maintained a highly successful lost and found service—still utilized by residents today—conducted educational talks to area schoolchildren, started a low-cost vaccination clinic, and sterilized and vaccinated literally thousands of animals. Although they experienced a fair share of controversy, criticism, and conflict with the community, the success of this organization was also certainly helped along by the timely arrival of Charlie Black, whom I discuss more in Chapter 5. Before we move into contemporary issues, I would like to give the backgrounds of two other groups in the community.

People's Anti-Cruelty Association/ Albuquerque Animal Rescue

One of the people who split from the Anti-Cruelty Federation shortly after they opened their new facility was a woman by the name of Irene Stockman. Even in the 1960s, before the philosophy was embraced on a national level and institutionalized by national groups, Irene believed that no healthy or treatable animal should be killed to control pet overpopulation.

Irene started her own group, the People's Anti-Cruelty Association (PACA), in 1973, housing animals on her own property in southwest Albuquerque. According to Jane Long, who has been with PACA since the early 1990s, adoption clinics were practically nonexistent in 1973, but Irene did manage to place some animals and accepted donations to support her rescue work. In 1991, several PACA volunteers organized to secure adoption clinics at local pet stores, which were beginning to endorse the goals of humane societies and place homeless animals in their stores for adoption. Jane explained that Irene as an owner/founder was not in a growth orientation, but as she grew older, other volunteers became concerned with how the animals on her property would be placed. These volunteers decided to form Albuquerque Animal Rescue (AAR), which became the adoption extension of PACA. AAR was successful in placing many of the animals Irene was holding at her home and it also began fostering strays for placement.

By the early 1990s, Irene's health was in decline. Because she was not considered a "business person," there were issues over bills and operations, which AAR attempted to take over once it was established. As she grew more frail, AAR volunteers began taking over more of the management of the group. Irene went into the hospital in winter in the late 1990s and never came out. According to Jane, on her deathbed Irene told her three children that she wanted everything to go to the organization, but she hadn't even made a will.

For years, neighbors who moved in around Irene's property in the South Valley, which was once rural, had complained about her animals. The city had made an agreement with Irene that as long as she lived, she could continue to keep those animals on her property. Once she died any animals still there had to be removed. She left her estate and thirty-seven dogs to the PACA/AAR. The volunteers pulled together to make a concerted effort to keep the organization afloat, despite the fact that the founder had died. They first had to get the animals into foster homes. The animals were moved to a local veterinary clinic and volunteers came by every evening to clean kennels and feed them in order to keep costs down. Jane said that she would get off work, and would clean kennels until 8:00 at night, and then go home and answer PACA voicemail. "It was like a second full-time job with no pay" (Long 1999). When volunteers entered Irene Stockman's home to find paperwork, they found it "filed" in four thirty-gallon garbage cans. Her checkbook recorded that the organization had exactly $12.48.

There was some dissension within the group about how the organization would be run after Stockman died, and some members left and formed their own organization. Jane and others in the group believed that the only way to be successful in helping animals was to conduct the organization as a business, even if it were a nonprofit business. They wanted to know how many animals were being fostered, how animals would be placed, and how much money was being used. The two members who disagreed and left to form their own group were later charged with animal neglect when they were found harboring about sixty animals they could not place in homes.

Of the animals cleared from Stockman's home, all but about six were placed with new families. Two were beyond medical attention and were euthanized, and four highly unsocialized animals were shipped to Best Friends, a no-kill animal sanctuary in Utah. PACA/AAR, completely run by volunteers, is still in existence today, and boasts a base of 125 volunteers. Each year, the group places about six hundred animals from foster care into new homes.

The basic philosophy of PACA/AAR, in the words of Jane Long, is that of the no-kill philosophy, which has become a national movement among humane welfare groups. PACA/AAR takes this a step further and tries to treat or rehabilitate, through foster care, animals before they will consider euthanasia. According to Jane, out of the six hundred animals they foster each year, only about 1 percent, or six, are killed. The procedure is performed by a veterinarian. The group conducts adoption clinics at various pet stores in town and has managed to increase its productivity over the past five years.

The Alliance against Animal Abuse

The Alliance is the youngest of the three groups I will discuss in this book. Unlike the other two groups, which have passed out of the hands of their founders to other committed volunteers and workers, the Alliance is still being managed and run by its originator, Barbara Tellier.

The Alliance differs from the other groups on several levels, though the two members I interviewed share the philosophies of traditional shelter work, including euthanasia. Barbara says she became involved in animal welfare in 1985, when her husband was on the road conducting business between El Paso and Las Cruces, a university town located in southern New Mexico. Along Interstate 25, he saw some thoroughbred horses outside of Truth or Consequences, New Mexico, and was concerned at how they appeared to be underweight. Barbara became involved by calling the state and county officials in Socorro County, but found that this county still did not possess an animal control division, even though state law mandated that every county in the state have one. After several days of phone calls, she couldn't find anyone with the legal authority to do something about the horses, which weren't getting enough food. So she called the *Albuquerque Journal* and asked them to run an article. The journalist assisted her by printing the names of all people she had spoken to who had failed to provide her with the means to assist these horses.

Barbara formed the Alliance against Animal Abuse (AAAA) and incorporated in October 1985. Although she started out concerned only with assisting horses, it quickly evolved into other humane concerns. Because she was the only nonprofit cruelty investigator in the state, she would travel into rural areas on complaints, and upon arriving at these places would find not only skinny horses, but quite saturated populations of dogs and cats as well. She implemented a low-cost spay/neuter program to offer to these people when she visited them to investigate their animals for cruelty and neglect.

Barbara has been involved with a number of cases of animal collectors and highly publicized conflicts with state, city, and county agencies over the enforcement of cruelty laws. The work she does differs in many ways from the work being performed at shelters and in foster care groups, although she herself does foster animals and places some for adoption. She and her volunteers investigate cruelty, offer spaying and neutering, and keep an eye on local officials to ensure that animals are well cared for under state and county laws. We will return to her and the other groups in the next two chapters, when I introduce the daily work environments, special cases, and the experiences and philosophies of the people and animals that work within the rescue and shelter system.

Conflict and Cooperation between Groups

The animal welfare movement is made up of people who firmly believe that animals do have rights. Whether this is merely the right not to suffer, or the right to be free from any pain or neglect, the right to live out their natural lives without human interference, or the right to live as nature intended them to live, there is a person who will defend one or all of these rights. Some of these people do so by sending money to charities that do this work. Some of them merely share their opinions with whoever happens to be near. Others volunteer their time. Some go so far as to write books on the movement, and some devote their lives, money, and homes, sacrificing personal happiness for the cause of animal rights.

As soon as people start to realize that they have common goals, they also realize that these goals differ along a continuum, as they do in any social movement. Just as there are varying degrees of feminist or environmental advocacy, so are there far greater degrees of difference among animal advocates. The media tends to blur these small distinctions, which is unfair to the activists, as it defeats many small changes by focusing on major ones to attract attention. I have met very few animal advocates who endorse the use of violence to liberate animals, even though many of them believe that cruelty to animals deserves harsh punishment. Some believe that anyone who has the ability to harm a child or a pet should be castrated and experimented upon, and while they outwardly discourage such tactics, they silently cheer when animals are rescued from labs or liberated from a puppy mill. I will admit that there have been times when I have become so angry at the person turning in a shivering, mournful ten-year-old dog that has never known any other life, to spend his final days in a shelter on a cold concrete floor, that I have cursed them and wished them the same ugly fate. I am not above frustration or petty anger, despite the fact that I have the benefit of distance through articulation. I am a victim of my own assumptions and prejudices, just as my co-workers are, and when I refer to them as a group, I include myself in that group. I always try to remember though, that all people are somewhere on a continuum when it comes to their relationships with animals, and that sometimes the most effective way to change their minds is to set a good example.

The original reason I chose to write a book on the animal welfare community in Albuquerque was because I was immediately struck by the number of animal welfare groups in this community, and then by the conflicts that arose as each group tried to do essentially the same thing. I noticed that the veterinary community did not always endorse the methods of population control that the shelters promoted, even though they were aware of the outcome of neglect and abuse. I realized that this lack of communication was a national problem in the animal welfare movement, and that people had already written books about it (Finsen and Finsen 1994; Francione 1996). Albuquerque is unique in my estimation because, while it contains a high level of conflict between groups, there are some workers who realize that the only way to solve the problem of pet overpopulation is to join forces and bring every strength to the table. This involves swallowing a fair amount of pride and aggravation. It involves holding back a passionate plea or a quick temper. It requires people to overcome ego and personality differences to work towards the end of unnecessary killing. It is a serious challenge on both a personal and professional level to adjust a lifetime of beliefs to find some common ground.

Not surprisingly, few people who truly care about animal-related issues are very successful at finding a way to communicate with one another. Even on national levels, there are thousands of groups applying themselves to very specific aspects of animal welfare and rescue work. I have also learned that these committed people cycle through the movement quite quickly, and that cooperation wanes and depends on the level of understanding and vision of those involved. Over the course of the six years I have been involved in writing this book, Albuquerque's humane movement has seen a few peaks and many more serious valleys.

What are the biggest conflicts among Albuquerque welfarists? Predictably, the most highly contested areas between nonprofit groups are euthanasia and funding. These two aspects of sheltering animals inter-twine and often work against the workers and animals, keeping divisions within the movement and presenting a confusing picture to the public. Abolitionists, such as Ingrid Newkirk of People for the Ethical Treatment of Animals (PETA), have argued against this division as it pertains to euthana-sia. Others, such as Tom Regan and Gary Francione, have lambasted the "New Welfarists," claiming that complacency and compromise are what truly harm the movement (Francione 1996; Newkirk 1991; Regan 1986). What some authors do not pay enough attention to is that even among welfarists there is a high degree of variance on what rights animals have, on how to best achieve those rights, and what people can actually do to change the centuries of unacceptable animal usage.

As more and more funding is channeled into groups that claim they do not kill healthy animals, "traditional" welfarists are becoming increasingly alarmed that killing animals will once again be left in the hands of people they view as callous and hardened (city workers)—or worse, the people who allow the animals to breed in the first place. This competition over funding becomes a battle over the meanings of quality versus quantity—over what the natural life of an animal is worth. As tra-ditional animal shelters struggle to create an image of business savvy and sophistication, other grass roots organizations move in to fill the space left by former "little old ladies in tennis shoes." City pounds continue to come under attack as contributing to animal cruelty and neglect by employing underpaid, burned-out, and poorly trained workers. High turnover and low pay in nonprofit organizations also result in a poorly trained, incom-petent work force, much to the alarm of committed volunteers who have remained with an organization through several cycles of staffing.

Which group is most successful at preventing animal neglect? What role does class play in these conflicts? How are the daily problems resolved? While I will not offer sound solutions to all of these issues, I believe the peo-ple involved in this work have some interesting points to make.

About a year after I started working at the Albuquerque shelter, several workers were called to investigate a possible abuse case in a nearby county. The county animal control officer did not feel he had sufficient ability or space to handle the sixty animals that were apparently living in various stages of neglect at this site. He enlisted the aid of several AHANM workers, including a part-time veterinarian who has been associated with more active welfare causes than many in this community. When they arrived at the scene, the veterinarian recognized the people living in the trailer as the managers of a small animal rescue group she had helped in the past. Unfortunately, something had gone terribly wrong with the group since she had seen them last. They had split from another group over philosophical differences and were trying to maintain about sixty dogs. Their adoption clinics had been somewhat unsuccessful because, they claimed, they were being squeezed out by the larger, better-funded groups. They were obviously completely overwhelmed.

When the investigators entered the property to search for injured or sick animals, they found the same conditions that other investigators find when they raid the homes of collectors. Feces and urine covered the floors, walls, counter tops, and beds. Animals were hidden in boxes and crates. Approximately twelve feline leukemia–positive cats were sharing two overflowing litter boxes. A dead animal was found in a shed with a makeshift IV thrown over a rafter. In the midst of this, the "rescuers" were walking around in their bare feet, accusing the representatives from the shelter of wanting to kill all of their animals.

In the end, when the case went before a judge, it was determined that these were well-intentioned, caring people who had simply become overwhelmed by caring for so many animals. Unwilling to compromise their pet-keeping philosophy, their stance against euthanasia kept them from seeking help from other, more established shelters. According to one of the workers who raided the site, the dogs were all friendly and many were highly adoptable (Husler personal communication). The problem was that they were hidden in the country with no way to get them into new homes. The irony of the situation for me was that these were the same two rescuers I had adopted Camille from several years before.

This case briefly had us discussing the differences between quality of life and quantity of life. I was a firm defender of euthanasia as a way to relieve suffering, and always had been. I recall one of the workers saying, "How do you teach people 'quality' of life?" Is it enough that they live, no matter what kind of environment or interaction they receive? Are animal sanctuaries that house hundreds of animals and maintain small staffs able to provide adequately for these highly social creatures? Many people believe not. The Albuquerque newspapers frequently cover cases of animal collecting, an investigative job that often falls to Barbara Tellier and the Alliance against Animal Abuse. Many of the offenders claim to be providing a safe haven for animals and manage to get contributions from unsuspecting citizens. When they are convicted of animal abuse they wait a few years and start all over again. According to Barbara, one of the collectors she has dealt with repeatedly over the years has been photographed lying face down on the ground in December, passed out from alcohol intoxication, while the animals in his care had no food or water (Tellier 1999). Her observation of some of these collectors is that they start with good intentions and become corrupted when they try to live off of the meager donations that come in for the animals. Like any addiction, the ability to resist collecting animals is difficult, and the recidivism rate is exceptionally high.

The HSUS web page (http:\\www.hsus.org) provides interested readers with articles regarding kill versus no-kill shelters. Julie Miller Dowling's article, "Unwanted Burden: Animal Shelters Debate the Role of Euthanasia," originally published in the *HSUS News*, Winter 1998, discusses the main points of this argument. Essentially, it does boil down to a debate over quality versus quantity, and as Dowling mentions, those same people that brought pet overpopulation to the forefront of the public's awareness are defending this method of controlling pet overpopulation to the same public. As she states, these workers are forced to defend euthanasia against "well-meaning animal advocates who portray euthanasia, rather than the problems necessitating euthanasia, as the evil" (Dowling 1998, 2). The HSUS advises limited (no-kill) admission shelters and open (kill) admission shelters to respect the roles each plays in communities, and to honor the responsibilities towards animals each group takes on (1998, 3). HSUS warns against using euthanasia as a fundraising tactic, which many limited admission shelters have done in the past. In addition, misrepresenting the pet overpopulation problem is a far more serious outcome of these arguments. Dowling presents the case of the San Francisco SPCA, which claims to have created the first "no-kill" community in the country. Unfortunately, the media often fails to explain that years of cooperation, planning, financial support, and the deaths of thousands of animals in other agencies went towards creating such a safe community for adoptable pets. Many communities have realized that cooperation is the only way to achieve this goal, but it is a cooperation not easily found among animal advocates in our society.

As soon as AHANM found property and established a facility, members left upon learning that animals would be euthanized if homes were not found for them. The veterinarian the Evanses had worked with in the past felt that euthanasia was not a solution to pet overpopulation, as did other members who went on to establish their own rescue groups. Thelma and Ed felt justified by the work they did, believing that providing a humane death to unadoptable animals was the only alternative they had at that time. "I know what I did, and that's what Ed and I used to say to each other. We'd analyze criticisms and agree, the two of us, that was the only alternative we had" (Evans 1999). Some of the critics of euthanasia and AHANM were later charged with animal collecting, and their animals were seized by the city because of the health and safety hazards they posed. Thelma tried to avoid working with other groups because of these philosophical differences, but the original distance she established has eased at AHANM in the years since she retired from the shelter.

After years of working for an open admission shelter, Joel Warner accepted a position at a no-kill shelter in Colorado. As he explained, he was "tired of killing." What he saw made him change his policy almost immediately. As soon as he turned away animals due to limited space, the same animals were found starving and dodging traffic on the side of the road. Animals that could not be adopted would suffer from illness in the kennels for an indeterminate amount of time. This experience led to his decision to eventually make this shelter an open admission shelter that euthanized animals.

Some of the workers of other groups do not euthanize animals, but not because they don't believe it is necessary. As Barbara Tellier, of AAAA, stated,

> That no-kill phrase is really cute, because . . . certain organizations in town advertise "Oh, enjoy the thrill of no-kill." Well, that's because when people call them, they say "Nope, can't take them, we're full." We've been keeping these two, 80-lb. siblings together for three years now because no one wants to adopt them together. So, you know he [another shelter manager] did say that, that is in his advertising and granted, he doesn't have a DEA license so he can't kill. But you take them to a facility that does. Basically that's what we do. It's not because I bring them here [to AHANM] to be killed, but I think they have a much better chance at adoption and I think [AHANM] can handle a lot more than I can in my backyard. (Tellier 1999)

Barbara believes that she is not as alarmed by the necessity to kill animals because she grew up on a farm and was used to seeing animals sacrificed for food or other purposes. She and her volunteers believe that spending $500 to mend a broken hip on an unadoptable stray is a misuse of funding, when that same money can spay ten to fifteen dogs or cats. Finally, she reiterates the commonly overlooked fact that euthanasia by these groups requires a veterinarian or other qualified professional to handle the drugs and administer the solution. Small grass roots groups can seldom afford this with their limited funding.

Jane Long explains what she means by the "thrill of no-kill" in these terms:

> I think it's that important, for the animals, for the people to come together. However I will maintain that if I'm representing my organization, which is very sensitive, this is a very sensitive issue to people who do traditional shelter work. . . . I will still promote my organization as no-kill because that's the philosophy that we adopt . . . and that's all it is. It doesn't make our work better or worse than traditional shelter work. . . . At any given time we could change. . . . AHA could change. All it is, is philosophy and things change. . . . It's becoming more and more prevalent with the no-kill philosophy that it's more of a philosophy people are willing to embrace. We've already done it the traditional way for 200 years in this country and it ain't working. There's still too many animals. But what would happen if the traditional people and the no-kill people came together, to create an environment to do all the right things for animals to actually reduce the number of animals out there?"

Author: "What would you propose?"

> Aggressive spay/neuter. Communities that can effectively go . . . no-kill, which is—you're euthanizing the minimum number of animals . . . for at least every single healthy animal that you handle is going to get a home. That's the first step to being no-kill. No healthy animal is put down. Now you've got a big span of "healthy." Then the next step is every treatable animal. . . .
>
> I don't have a right to sit here and go "Boy, I'm great, I'm doing no-kill work." The only reason I can do that no-kill work is because the city and AHA are actually taking care of the excess animals. We can't. Five and six hundred animals a year is nothing in the big picture of things, when you realize that probably 50,000 animals are going to be put down here this year. (Long 1999)

Kelly Chapel, who works for three groups (four if we include her Pug Rescue), had this to say about dealing with different philosophies:

The fact of it is, there aren't enough homes for all of them. I wish to God we didn't have to [euthanize] but until we get all these morons to spay and neuter. . . . As a matter of fact, my foster puppies' mom got put to sleep. I figured that she would, she's a little black dog, no manners, nothing special, just a little black dog. . . .

I got in a pretty big argument with —— [a volunteer at AHANM]. . . . I don't like putting these animals to sleep but I understand it, and if I'm going to be a volunteer over there [AHANM] I am not going to run around badmouthing you. Nobody likes it. It really made me mad. I heard her say, "Well I heard them say that they wouldn't even take a nine-year-old rottweiler." And I looked at her and I said, "Would you adopt a nine-year-old rottweiler?" "Well, yes, I would," she said, " I adopted an eleven-year-old cocker spaniel." And I said, "You know, there's a little bit of difference between a nine-year-old rottweiler and an eleven-year-old cocker spaniel." I mean, come on here. . . . She said, "I don't think that they should be doing that. They should at least give them a chance," and I'm like, "There is no chance, babe. These people that come in off the street are not going to go pay $75 for a nine-year-old rottweiler that they don't have any idea what he's been through all his life." (Chapel 1999)

She goes on to explain that other groups can't take such highly unadoptable animals because they are already full with adoptable ones. Kelly also endorses aggressive spay/neuter programs as the only truly viable solution to pet overpopulation. Kelly is not unique in her use of different groups for different animals. At the time of this interview, she was trying to find a home through PACA for a dog that had been considered unadoptable at the traditional shelter because it had snapped at a child. She believed she could find an adequate home that didn't have any children in it. Beth Petronis also mentioned adopting animals she found through other groups if she believed they had little chance at AHANM (Chapel 1999; Petronis 1999). At that time, neither group had a problem with this shuffling, because both of these women respected the different functions each group served in the community and the managers of the shelters respected the time and resources these women contributed to their efforts.

Workers who have only been exposed to one group, such as those at AHANM, tend only to see the conflicts that exist. This is no fault of their own, but it does tend to accentuate the features of other groups that create tension. Accepting animals all day at an open admission shelter leads to some degree of cynicism, but when word reaches these workers that their efforts are being sabotaged or criticized, they become frustrated that their efforts are being mis-construed. A common statement to be directed at staff from some volunteers and definitely from clients at the traditional shelter is, "Call us if anything bad is going to happen." Cynthia Baca's response to this is, "Well, you know what? Something bad happens every day!" When groups hold adoption clinics at the same site, tensions are easily discerned by observers. Susan Brannock occa-sionally worked alongside another group that resisted being interviewed for this book, and had this to say about the experience:

> The first Saturday that they were there, no one at their booth would speak to me. I just don't put up with that from people so the next time they were there . . . I told them that I thought we were here for the same reason. "I'm interested in finding homes for homeless animals and saving lives, as, obviously, are you. You obviously have some sort of problems or difference with either me or Animal Humane and I'd really like to know what it is." And that's basically how I tried to start a conversa-tion. (Brannock 1999)

She found that by talking to the members of this group that they did differ over the need for euthanasia, but after hearing Susan's side of it some of them began to understand that it was necessary in some cases. Their biggest problem, according to Susan, was the level of bad informa-tion they had received from unreliable sources. According to Susan, this resulted from innuendo and rumors that groups passed around in compe-tition with other groups—competition that often arose over funding.

Jane Long commented on the fact that even groups with surface similarities may have some philosophical differences that create occasional animosity. The same group Susan mentioned, according to Jane, can be difficult to work with at times because they are unwilling to accept new technologies or ideas. So even though their philosophies are almost exactly alike regarding euthanasia, Jane sees her organization as more willing to try new techniques to reach more adopters. This includes mobile adoptions, early age spay/neuters, and accepting a certain amount of business savvy to run the organization.

An interesting event occurs when these groups do come together for a major Adoptathon, held every year the first weekend in May. The larger shelters organize the event, but smaller groups are invited to participate as long as they contribute a substantial fee to pay for the expenses incurred. In 1999, it was suggested that in order to avoid confusion, the adoption questionnaires from all of the groups be broken down into one document that encompassed the major questions from all. The original questionnaires were already nearly identical. The adoptions manager at the traditional shelter, Tracy Ploor, produced a document she felt was fair and equitable, and it was accepted by the other groups prior to the event. Unfortunately, when the event did arrive, some members of the smaller no-kill groups rejected the form in favor of their original questionnaires, and they stiffly informed volunteers from other groups not to counsel people regarding their animals. In my opinion, the degree of connection with the animals is what produces this feeling of strict control over the home it will go into. When you foster an animal in your own home, you get to know it better than if you only see it in passing at work. Although their protective attitudes can be understood, it didn't exactly create an atmosphere of cooperation between other groups, who viewed these actions as another instance of criticism of varying methods.

Tracy had this to say about the differences between group philosophies:

> I'm willing to live and let live. We exist too. Not everyone wants to bring an animal to a shelter that euthanizes, and they have these other options and they're welcome to investigate them. If they can follow through with what those other organizations are asking them to do in order to get this animal to them, good for them! Please, do that! A lot of people come back to us because they couldn't get into those places or they couldn't do what they required, or it wasn't the proper animal to take to those places. . . . I didn't realize that they would pick and choose what they would take and what they couldn't. (Ploor 1999)

Tracy goes on to say that though her initial reaction to these philosophies was poor, she has since met several representatives of these groups and finds them to be "nice people with good intentions." She finds it difficult when they rely on the traditional shelter's high visibility and high funding to promote their own animals or philosophies, and then they bad mouth the traditional shelter for euthanizing. She states, "It's like religion. There are so many different religions, but they're all trying to get to the same place. Let 'em do it. There's a different path for everybody" (Ploor 1999).

Tracy has also had problems with other groups who misrepresent themselves to the public and then bring the seized animals to AHANM. Other groups rely on AHANM's and Animal Services' resources—such as euthanasia, veterinary care, and donated food—and then complain about the policies the shelters endorse to the public, and in some cases sue over philosophical differences. Many of the people I interviewed mentioned that it is of utmost importance that any animal group not lie to the public about the possible final outcome for the animals they rescue. Unfortunately, omission is sometimes the way these groups avoid being lumped with shelters that euthanize, as Dowling suggests has happened in cities like San Francisco.

Many shelters maintain requirements of what they can accept, how many animals they can accept a day, and then, obviously, what happens to them after that. My only criticism of this practice is that I believe we do not simply judge an animal by what it looks like to us. Instead, we construct categories for animals based on all the surrounding information. As Tracy stated, "A lot of the impression of that animal . . . comes from the people who bring it in" (Ploor 1999). This impression is certainly based on what those people say and do, how they dress, what they drive, and how they speak. In my opinion, animal welfare groups can unknowingly defeat their own educational goals by only working with a select group of clients. This is not a trait that is unique to any group in this community—it is highly stratified and that stratification is rarely challenged by anyone. With regards to volume, Animal Services (the city pound) is required to take everything that walks in the door. AHANM would be the next step up, followed in varying degrees by the other rescue groups, depending on which population they focus their efforts on. Each group, except for Animal Services, employs a screening process before animals are accepted. And in the case of those groups that are supposed to serve the same populations, there are increased conflicts and criticisms over how the populations are educated and how the animals should be handled.

I also found this to be true in Kentucky, but to a lesser degree because there are fewer rescue groups serving the smaller community of Louisville. The Kentucky Humane Society never turned any animal away from its doors, but due to a city ordinance, if the animal was a stray and not highly adoptable, it would be transferred to the city pound for its stray holding period. This ordinance, which was probably intended to make it easier for people to claim their pets, had negative effects on the animals. At the time of my research (1998), the city pound in Louisville still euthanized adult animals using the gas chamber. No group in town maintained a rigorous or successful lost and found service, and therefore animals had fewer opportunities to be returned to their original owners. The workers at the shelter there agreed with me that this was deplorable, and they mentioned that they had attempted to train city workers to euthanize by injection. For some reason, those workers preferred to rely on a method of euthanasia that has been successfully phased out of most urban communities in other regions of the country (including shelters in the South), and I have never heard any citizen of that city complain about the method. Most people I mention it to are not even aware that the gas chamber is used or that it has been considered less humane than other methods. Obviously, an ethnography of this community would be an entirely different story from the evolution of Albuquerque's community, though it may have some similar themes. Louisville's use of technology to facilitate humane treatment of animals simply lags behind Albuquerque's by about twenty years.

The people I interviewed in Albuquerque had various degrees of affiliation with other animal-related causes, such as vegetarianism, breeding purebreds, owning horses, etc. These issues also fall along a continuum, with many people choosing which causes they can and cannot support. It appeared that higher degrees of extreme opinions regarding animals' rights surfaced in the smaller groups, while workers and staff from traditional shelters, though conscious of factory farming and opposed to cosmetic testing and fur wearing, maintained a more mainstream, less radical view of animal use. The concept of stewardship, as I have previously mentioned, surfaced repeatedly in conversations with these workers, while the volunteers from other groups seemed more concerned with issues such as the abolition of circus and display animals (zoos and museums) and the use of animals in research and food. Many of the people I interviewed came from rural backgrounds and believed in gentle usage. Others explained to me that they felt a kinship living with other carnivores, and used this as a defense of meat eating.

Some of the primary figures in the extreme movement have criticized the use of euthanasia by traditional shelters as a means of population control. Tom Regan spends a considerable amount of time making it clear that the deaths that are experienced by animals in shelters are not mercy killings, per se, because the animals are often healthy. He believes that this method of killing should not, therefore, be called "euthanasia" (Regan

1983, 114–116). According to most of the individuals I interviewed, including the people who actually administer the shot, it truly is killing, and in exclusive company that is exactly what they call it. They reserve the term "euthanasia" for use with the general public, which is likely to find them callous and insensitive when they mention "killing" animals. Many times workers, in an obvious attempt to avoid euthanizing healthy animals, justified killing them as soon as animals showed any sign of upper respiratory infections—which are nearly unavoidable in a group kennel. Some animals were even euthanized for upper respiratory infections when they became hoarse from barking.

In spite of the many differences between the individuals who belong to these groups, there has been an effort in recent years to form coalitions with the goal of decreasing the euthanasia and abuse rates in New Mexico. Progressive pet businesses have seen this as a lucrative market and have invited shelters to offer their animals for adoption, as opposed to breeders and puppy mills. These coalitions are certainly not without conflict in themselves, but they seem to be developing with the understanding that euthanasia as a means of population control has its repercussions. The most recent of these coalitions was designed by an animal advocacy group called Animal Protection of New Mexico (APNM). Over the Internet, I interviewed the coordinator of this group, Helga Schimkat. I present in her own words the responses to my questions regarding the No More Homeless Pets Coalition:

> In early 1999 APNM became aware of the surge in interest across the country in attacking so called surplus animal or pet overpopulation problems. At the same time substantial funds were being made available to certain kinds of cooperative projects dealing with those issues. . . . Although many organizations were and have continued to address cat and dog overpopulation, APNM felt that the problem could now begin to be attacked seriously because of the prospects for large-scale funding—a necessity when dealing with so many surplus animals. Because APNM is a statewide organization and has worked with many of the animal organizations in New Mexico, including creating other successful coalitions, we believed that New Mexico had the potential to create a successful coalition of organizations, agencies and individuals to tackle the problems of our state having too many cats and dogs and not enough homes.

The No More Homeless Pets Coalition exists to work on decreasing the dog and cat overpopulation in New Mexico—period. We may apply for [funding] at some point but that is not our sole reason for working together.

The coalition's mission statement is "to eliminate the killing of dogs and cats as a solution for pet overpopulation." The coalition intends to accomplish that mission by decreasing the number of dogs and cats born each year and increasing the number of dogs and cats that find good homes. The coalition will attain that goal by implementing aggressive spay/neuter and adoption programs. Although the coalition does not intend to force animal shelters in New Mexico to become "no-kill" shelters, the coalition expects that as a result of the coalition's work over the next several years, animal shelters will no longer need to euthanize healthy, adoptable dogs and cats.

We have found interest and participation in the coalition to be overwhelmingly positive. We have had about 30 organizations join or at least participate in one or more meetings. Participation has been across the board from large scale city run shelters and animal control agencies to grass roots organizations with only [one] or two volunteers running the group. (Schimkat 2000)

In order for these aggressive spay/neuter programs to work, entire communities will need to recognize the problem of animal overpopulation and do what they can to prevent it. This means that veterinarians, breeders, shelter workers, animal control officers, city officials, and pet owners will need to take their share of responsibility for the disposal or placement of unwanted pets.

Low-cost veterinary clinics offer affordable services to those classes of people that the many humane societies target as the root of the overpopulation problem, but very seldom do shelters make an attempt to alter the habits of people in other social classes. Albuquerque is unique among other cities, because there is a city ordinance that requires breeders to display a license when advertising their puppies. The same ordinance prohibits the selling or giving away of animals without a license (Albuquerque Animal Control Ordinance 1999, 10). It is highly doubtful that many people outside of the welfare community have any knowledge of this law. The newspapers for some time were requiring people to display their breeder's license number when advertising their animals, but have since stopped.

Having laws on the books is one thing; getting them enforced is quite another. According to defenders of the enforcement agency, there is simply not enough funding to keep it enforced.

Although humane educational programs have been criticized as being ineffective, this is simply another area of traditional shelter work that requires some change. The Internet has become a useful vehicle for advertising pets and providing lost and found services. Youth-intervention programs, which teach children how to care for and train pets, can have tremendous effects on the future of shelter work by creating a base of people in the community who can train and properly care for dogs. This skill could have a fan effect, placing skilled dog trainers in each sub-community of the city. Holding these training camps at an animal shelter allows children to understand the tragic outcome of improper treatment of animals. The one program at the Kentucky Humane Society that truly inspired me was the educational camp it held in the summer, where dozens of children worked at the shelter for a week and learned about humane issues. It is my opinion that legislation which makes humane and environmental issues part of the public school curriculum—not just a once-a-year, one-hour speech from a humane educator—could have the same therapeutic and long-term effects on this country's youth as art, music, and creative writing programs.

The animal welfare community in Albuquerque is more than fifty years old and carries with it themes of strong personalities, people motivated by a sense of obligation and moral duty, and, at times, the willingness to pool their resources and overcome individual differences for the good of companion animals. Tracing the history of animal welfare on international, national, and local levels allows us to view the human–companion animal bond as one that is closely tied to the morality of the time. Humane societies strongly affect how that history will develop by making their concerns a part of public morality. We can see how these themes have danced around the incorporation of animals as pseudo-members of our own families. Nevertheless, there are still those behaviors we cannot completely control, namely sexuality and those instinctual behaviors that do not integrate into our lives—that keep us from completely constructing an animal and removing it from nature or from itself. Although many of those behaviors that cause animals to be left in shelters are considered "natural" for dogs, humane societies have successfully convinced our culture that these behaviors must be modified or eliminated for a dog to become a companion animal. They can, in most cases, be tempered by sterilization and training. The question arises, Are the animals involved in this construction at all? Which

Colonel Evans and other members of AHANM, circa 1970s.

Photo courtesy of AHANM

has the overriding effect—our culture, or their nature? Is this our species' uncomfortable legacy of domestication, or is the evolutionary pay-off for animals worth their immediate discomforts? As Yi Fu Tuan stated, pets offer us the ability to show the best and worst behavior toward another social being that we can exhibit or imagine. In keeping with that belief, dogs are most certainly the closest reflections to ourselves in nature with whom we have formed a bond.

In the next chapter we will meet some of the people who compose the stories of animals' lives while they are in between identification with a permanent family.

"This One Mattered to Me . . ."

Every day, an old man walked the beach with a pail, picking up starfish that had been washed in by the tide, and throwing them back into the sea. One day a young boy stopped the old man and asked, "Why do you throw the starfish back? It doesn't matter. They will only wash up on the shore again tomorrow."

The old man picked a starfish out of his pail, and threw it as far as he could into the sea and replied, "It mattered to this one." (author unknown)

A woman who has worked tirelessly for animal welfare in Albuquerque shared this wonderful parable with me. A gold starfish pin accompanied it, to remind me that the work we do doesn't change the entire world, but it can change the world of one individual. In this chapter, I will introduce several individuals who have made an impact on the welfare of animals—some in small ways, others in larger, more obvious ways. Their stories are shaped by the acquaintanceships and friendships they have developed with the animals in their care over the course of their work in this field.

Arnold Arluke, a sociologist, originally opened this field of inquiry with several excellent analyses of institutional animal care. In 1996, he brought several previously published articles together into a book called *Regarding Animals*, co-authored with fellow sociologist Clinton R. Sanders. In *Regarding Animals*, we are introduced to the conflicts and contradictions inherent in traditional shelter work and the use of animals in experimental labs. Yi Fu Tuan's observation that our relationships with companion animals are fraught with a strong dose of cruelty and sentimentality find a practical presentation in Arluke's ethnographic research.

Arluke noted that people in the lower-paying levels of animal care in both shelters and labs are drawn to the work often out of a "love" for animals and a desire to work with them. This desire to care for them is then challenged by the fact that in both of these environments animals are routinely sacrificed for some higher institutional purpose—either to decrease population, prevent future suffering, or perform experiments (1996, 82–131). Therefore, these individuals are required to develop some method of managing the stress of euthanizing the animals they become attached to. Arluke calls this the "caring/killing paradox" (1996, 85). He suggests that through a process of incorporation, workers develop strategies for resisting attachment to the animals that may have to be sacrificed. Some of these strategies include relying on shelter rhetoric to justify euthanasia and population control, focusing on shelter mascots, carefully choosing which animals to become attached to, and finally categorizing the shelter animals in a way that does not typically confuse emotional boundaries. What Arluke suggests is that shelter workers categorize the animals in the kennel as "virtual pets," existing almost in limbo, both on a physical plane as shelter residents, and emotionally to the workers. He maintains that workers come to view these animals as existing on a liminal plane somewhere between "pet and object" (1996, 86), "a population of refugees rather than as individual pets" (1996, 149).

My suggestion is that in shelters the category of potential "pet" may indeed *be* the place where most of these animals exist, with the attached subcategory of "rescue" or "abused" or "shelter" tacked on to further define their social positions. A pet, in itself, can be neither subject (on the emotional level of human family members) nor object (on the emotional level of property); it continually exists in a blurred category between these positions and relies heavily on its relationship to people. This blurred category makes it obvious why pets are so often the source of controversy and discussion in legal battles. They are not merely property, especially when it comes to the experience of neglect or cruelty, but neither can they defend themselves in a legal system in the true understanding of subjecthood and sense of self-will and motivation. Like it or not, they will almost always require the skills of a translator or defender in order to obtain rights (meaning at the very least the right not to suffer). In all other areas as well—food production, entertainment, scientific experimentation—animals occupy blurred categories and can never be fixed as either subject or object. They can be both to some people and can be one or the other at different times. What I am suggesting here is that pets and animals occupy a category of their own, one that does not imply extremes in subjection or objectification, but incorporates and rejects both. This proposal resists the tendency to group them into an either/or category, just as it resists the necessity to imply that the only place they can exist is in any given category.

This does not mean that I don't believe animals exhibit a strong sense of individuality and have an experience of self-consciousness. What I would suggest is that, in general, the *expression of selfhood* in animals relies on the bond an animal has with the people or persons who also experience that animal. An animal does experience itself, and it does experience its environment. However, as *Other*, they exist only in generalities, much as members of our own species exist for us if we are unfamiliar with their customs, language, and culture.

There are people who are trained to recognize the "language," or nature, of animals. Some of these only understand the languages of their personal pets, or of a specific breed. Trainers and veterinarians learn to understand and convey focused aspects of those languages—medical and behavioral. People who perform rescue and shelter work not only learn to recognize the language of abuse, neglect, comfort, and need, they also take these messages and use them to promote political, social, and moral agendas (the incorporation of animals into families). Therefore, when an animal reaches a shelter, it is still a pet, but how humans experience its "pethood" relies heavily on its resistance to incorporation and the construction of its victimhood and suffering. It is neither subject nor object, but a great deal of both, in addition to occupying a subcategory uniquely its own.

I am suggesting that the category of "pet" is a dynamic exchange of subjectivity and objectivity, sometimes throughout the life of one animal. In this, I believe Arluke and I agree. His summary to the chapter on shelter work in *Regarding Animals* states his belief that animals exist in uncomfortable, inconsistent categories in our culture, and that shelter workers are in a specialized setting that even further dramatizes those inconsistencies. While many of us experience these feelings occasionally in our lives, shelter workers learn to manage them every day (Arluke and Sanders 1996, 106). In addition, these workers are forced to find some justification for killing the animals that are not incorporated into families through adoption.

My observations differ from Arluke's research on this point. He suggests that when workers are first introduced to shelter work, they are subjected to a form of indoctrination that transforms them from people who love animals to people who kill them (and therein lies the paradox).

He implies that in order to kill certain animals, these workers must maintain an emotional distance from them. Based on my relationships and personal knowledge of these workers, I will suggest that it is nearly impossible for many of them to do so. It is my belief that the relationships workers develop with the animals in their care is far more complex and contextual to apply generalized concepts to that bond. In some cases, it is the level of empathy, intensified by the personal experiences of those workers, which allows them the justification for killing *based* on caring. Workers still maintain some distance from certain animals, and they allow themselves to become attached to others. They protect animals that they temporarily bond with, while maintaining a disinterest in others. It is more common for volunteers to notice the details and subtleties in many shelter animals, and this leads some volunteers to working with smaller, no-kill groups that only maintain relationships with a limited number of animals at a time. Many volunteers and workers foster underage or special needs animals as a means of obtaining emotional permission to bond with shelter animals. In the end, their inconsistent feelings towards euthanasia are informed by the ways in which they experientially relate to these marginalized animals.

For purposes of this study, I conducted formal interviews with twenty-five people. The majority of the interviewees (nineteen) were women. Five of the people interviewed were volunteers with various organizations, some affiliated with more than one group at any time. The other eighteen were employees or former employees at traditional shelters, and one was the founding member of her own organization. In addition to the interviews with groups in Albuquerque, I conducted several contrasting interviews with workers at a traditional shelter in Louisville, Kentucky. Due to limitations on time, resources, and distance, I was unable to include historical data on the Kentucky shelter or interview members of other groups in that city. The experience of working with these individuals provided valuable insight for the completion of this project and for a comparative view of the Albuquerque animal welfare community.

The people who volunteered to participate in this study did so enthusiastically. Though I had hoped to meet with many others, due to time restraints I had to be content with the twenty-five interviews I did conduct. I interviewed representatives from four groups in Albuquerque, including the Animal Humane Association of New Mexico (AHANM), People's Anti-Cruelty Association (PACA), the Alliance against Animal Abuse (AAAA), and the Coalition for No More Homeless Pets. I also interviewed a number of workers at the Kentucky Humane Society, but time constraints prevented me from incorporating those interviews in this text. They served instead as comparisons to the Albuquerque interviews.

People are drawn to shelter work because they have a strong desire to help animals, but in some cases this desire stems from personal experiences. As the next three stories relate, at times workers shelter animals because of a debt they feel they owe them. Beth Petronis, a very active volunteer at the traditional shelter, was a biology major in college and had a somewhat different experience of animals prior to volunteering her time at the shelter.

> I think what I'm doing now is, to some degree, atonement for the myriad of animals that we did just horrible research on in my undergraduate program, although there weren't that many, most were already dead. . . . We had to dissect cats, and dolphins, and sharks, and dogs and everything. And then we did live experiments in my animal physiology classes on rabbits and cats and dogs and that was pretty awful because there was no way that these animals could survive. And even pithing a frog now to me is, like, oh how did I ever do that? And I really think about those situations a lot . . . any animal I have a little hand in postponing a death . . . maybe I'm getting rid of some bad karma. I've never been one to purposefully hurt an animal, but in that context I didn't really have a choice. (Petronis 1999)

Susan Brannock also felt she had a debt to repay and found that working in a shelter would provide her with that opportunity.

> A lot of it is because of my dog . . . my big stupid dog that I got when I was very, very ill, and what he did for me. . . . I got this big stupid dog when I was just out of the hospital and having severe neurological problems and falling a lot and I fell on my big, soft dog repeatedly and thought he was the dumbest dog in the world because he wouldn't move and then I realized he was there on purpose. . . . He did good things for my heart and my soul and made me feel so good inside. And when I started doing better otherwise I just felt like I just had to find a way to do something back. (Brannock 1999)

Mike Hall, a kennel worker at AHANM who was in the Army for five years, told the following story. During a parachuting exercise, he was badly injured and as his story illustrates, he felt he had a great debt to repay for his life.

> If it wasn't for a German shepherd I wouldn't be here right now. . . . When I had my accident, I fell into a patch of forest that was too thick for people to even walk through. So after two days of lying there, I remember waking up one morning—I could feel my face and that's all I could feel. Couldn't feel my legs, I couldn't feel my body. I felt a German shepherd licking my face. That dog had found me in the woods. If it hadn't been for that dog they wouldn't have found me. That dog saved my life. From that point on I said, "Screw the Army." I had the option of going back in, but I said, "Screw it! This [animals] is what I really care about." (Hall 1999)

These three anecdotes narrate the motivation behind a great deal of rescue and shelter work. These workers feel they owe their lives, a greater awareness, or some sort of debt to animals, and working towards their welfare is a way to return that kindness. Other workers are drawn into more serious commitments to animal welfare after they start volunteering for a few hours a week, and then increase this time to nearly a full-time position (Golden; Lewis; Petronis; Ploor; Taborelli). I was recruited from the volunteer pool when I started working at AHANM, as were several of the people I interviewed. Kelly Chapel, an extraordinary volunteer who works as a full-time teacher, divides her time between three groups (AHANM, AAAA, and PACA) and also performs a breed rescue on her own. She was drawn to rescue work by a sense of injustice that moved her to action.

> I read an article in the paper that they had the animal shelter in Belen at the dump. No heat, no shade, just freezing cold, no real shelter, it was just a tin lean-to. It just infuriated me. It upset me so bad. I was hearing that they would go over there and do target practice on them. So I just, you know, that's when I got started. . . . When I first started this, I'd see a litter of puppies and I'd think, "Oh, how cute, and how nice they're giving them away at Wal-Mart. They're all going to get homes." And now I want to cry when I see them because it's so heartbreaking. Where are you going to end up? On the end of a chain, chained as far away from the house as they can possibly get you? (Chapel 1999)[1]

Other volunteers and workers were called to service by an interaction with a particular animal, as in the case with Marcy Britton, a volunteer with AAAA. Although her mother did some campaigning against the use of the gas chamber in California in the late 1960s and early 1970s, at that time Marcy was too young to really have an interest in animal welfare. Then shortly after she got her driver's license, she found a stray dog. She worked for two hours to get the dog into her vehicle, took the animal to the vet, paid over $200 to treat him, and then boarded him with the veterinarian until she could find him a home. Thinking that she had found the dog a *good* home, she called the adopters the next day, only to learn that the dog had "disappeared" overnight. Marcy states that was the last time she placed an animal on her own. From that moment on she took them to shelters or the pound. In her opinion, the pound was better than a life on the street, and she jokingly (not really) explained that she still allows herself an hour or so when she leaves the house in anticipation of finding a stray (Britton 1999).

These stories illustrate that, for a variety of reasons, what begins as sometimes a casual rescue or interest in saving one animal or donating some time turns into a more serious commitment.[2] This is obviously not true for all volunteers, but for the majority of those interviewed, animal welfare and rescue can easily become an all-consuming passion. I remember having a discussion with Kelly one day in which she more or less told me, "If I can't do this work, I don't know what I'll do! I *have* to help those animals!" (Chapel personal communication). Another interesting aspect of these stories is that animals are not always portrayed in them as victims. In the stories told by Susan and Mike, individual animals had performed some significant, sometimes heroic action that motivated these people to feel they had to work with other animals that needed human help. It was an exchange of kindness that predicated their interest in animal welfare.

My own life history has been a constant exchange with animals. Indeed, as most animal lovers can attest, I tend to demarcate major events of my life by which animal was present during it. Animals have also played a part in every major decision I have made or event that has happened to me. As a child, I drew pictures of the animals I knew and of the horses I knew only in my imagination. I wrote about animals from the tender age of six, when I dictated an article to my first-grade teacher for the school newspaper. It was about the series of cats my family had owned and how each had met its tragic end, either from car accidents to accidental suffocation or poisoning. My first poem was a four-line rhyme about losing my cat to a car when I was eleven. In retrospect, a compassion for the suffering of

my pets determined how my history would evolve, and the tragedy of losing those cats may have even determined how I have chosen to express my
connection with animals. I had never volunteered for any other group until
the time I started volunteering at AHA. I felt that I had found a home away
from home where I truly belonged and could make a real difference.
Writing this book is simply a continuation of that ten-line article I wrote in
first grade, a way for me to express the grief of losing those connections as
a child, and to be sure I maintained them as an adult.

　　　Barbara Tellier and Thelma Evans both grew up in rural communities on farms that held a variety of animals, and they were accustomed to
the activities associated with keeping livestock, such as castration and
butchering. Other people stated that they had always brought home strays
as children. I recall one worker telling me that she knew she was bound for
animal welfare work when, as a child, she rescued a litter of skunks (Husler
personal communication). In some cases, those rescued animals would be
taken to the pound by parents as soon as they came home (Tanner 1999).
Several of the people also stated that they had an intense and lengthy bond
with one special pet nearly throughout their entire childhood. Paula
Golden's childhood pet was a cocker spaniel cross named Cinnamon, who
lived with her family from the time Paula was seven to nineteen years old.
Susie Lewis, volunteer coordinator at AHANM, described her childhood
dog, Herbie, as "the love of my life." She had Herbie for thirteen years. Susan
Brannock reported that because she came from a military family, she was
not allowed to have pets as a kid. While working the front desk at the traditional shelter, she has the most difficulty taking in those animals that
come from military families who are suddenly transferred and can't take
them along. Tracy Ploor, the office manager for the traditional shelter, said
that her first dog, Betsy, was a terri-poo her family adopted from the pound.
Because Tracy's father grew up on a farm,[3] Betsy started out living outside.
Eventually, Betsy "was sitting at the table eating dinner with us!" Betsy lived
for sixteen years with the Ploor family.

　　　When I asked these folks how their families felt about the work they
did, I got almost the same response from everyone. It was quite common for
their families to misunderstand what motivated them to work with animals—especially considering the harder aspects of the work, such as rescue,
dealing with aggressive or dirty animals, and euthanasia. This was most
apparent for the people who worked at the traditional shelter, because quite
often their families did not support euthanasia. Others reported that their
parents worried that the animals they dealt with were dangerous or diseased.

"Out of all these years [13] I haven't gotten anything; no ringworm, no nothing! I've only been bitten once enough to be sent to the doctor" (Tanner 1999). One worker reported that her mother was somewhat confused about why her daughter would take a low-paying customer service job at a shelter when she had a degree from Yale. She responded by simply saying, "Well, I like it." Tracy described her relationship to her job by saying, "My passion is my work, and I throw myself into it. Maybe as I get older I'll grow into something else. . . . We all do our part, and this is my little part" (Ploor 1999).

Working with animals, for me, has been an obvious extension from my childhood, as I'm sure it was for many of the people I spoke with. After my mother remarried I was only allowed to have outside cats. For a couple of years I begged for a dog of my own, but I was told it was too much responsibility. I tease my mother now (who, by the way, since her divorce, has managed to acquire two dogs, four cats, and three rabbits) that the reason I got into this work was because she denied me a dog as child. It's also obvious that I inherited a love of animals from my parents, including my stepmother, who had a very close relationship with her Brittany spaniel, Danny. Although the pets I grew up with had different levels of interaction in my two family settings, they seemed to always be present in my life. When I was confirmed in the Catholic Church at fourteen, I chose Francis as my confirmation name, upon my mother's suggestion, because, as she told me then, he loved the little animals, "just like we do."

A portrait and a statue of St. Francis of Assisi have always adorned the front office of AHANM, and the idea that helping animals is a "calling" seems to feature prominently in the stories of why people are drawn to this work. A connection with a "higher" or more spiritual purpose appears to give these individuals the strength to hold to their convictions in spite of many daily setbacks. As Susan Brannock stated,

> I think one of the things that makes it easier to work here than it does for some people is the fact that I have my religious beliefs. . . . I see the situation with animals and overpopulation and human irresponsibility as one of the symptoms of a very sick society, I don't feel that I personally am going to change that. I look more at what I can do for this specific animal, this specific day, or this person on this day . . . a lot of times I see that people who really think they can change it and make an impact right now are sometimes the ones that really burn out quickly because no one person can change the whole [world]. (Brannock 1999)

In other words, *it mattered to this one*. And for many of these people, that one, or even just one a day, is enough to keep them from becoming overwhelmed.

I was interested in whether the initial experience of working in
shelters met with the subjects' previous conceptions of what shelters were
like. For some reason, I can't recall being particularly surprised by the number of animals that died, or by the callousness of the public. I was surprised
by the dedication of some of the volunteers and workers, and later I
became surprised when I visited other shelters—which I do whenever I
travel—and found that they did not view animals in the same light as my
peers in Albuquerque. I remember being in one shelter and hearing animals there being referred to as having a "shelf-life," meaning that they had
only a limited time to be adoptable/marketable. This appalling use of business rhetoric and objectification seemed to only undermine any efforts the
welfare movement was making to convince laypeople of the sentience of
companion animals. I have been equally appalled when shelter administrators offer the public free bags of dog food as an incentive to adopt, even
though I have resorted to these tactics myself in order to place a particularly promising animal. Although the "shelf-life" statement may have been
taken out of context, it is surprising when the practitioners in the field
seem to have difficulty defining exactly what it is that they do and especially *why they do it*. I heard another individual refer to shelter animals as
"used cars"—specifically as "lemons"—although he did so in a manner
that conveyed his sympathy to the listener, while relying on a metaphor
that relayed how tragic it was that animals could be thought of as used cars.
This language play is an interesting and unique quality of working in these
fields, and could provide a rich area for further study, especially as language
relates to the categorization of animals and pets. Arluke notes that learned
"mottos" are commonplace in shelter culture (1996, 87). Throughout his
essay, I read phrases and "daily affirmations" that I was taught during my
own incorporation and that I heard over and over during my interviews.
Verbal play, black humor, categorization, talking to and about the animals
("dogese" or "doggeral") relay a great deal of information about how those
animals are experienced by the workers.

A common phrase heard in any animal shelter is "I don't work
here to get rich!" This implies that the only reason to work in a nonprofit
job involving animals is because you are motivated to help animals and
not to make money. Most of the workers I interviewed for this project were
either volunteers or had started their jobs at the shelters making minimum

wage. As can be expected, even individuals in management positions cannot boast of significant salaries. As a matter of fact, many national organizations have come under criticism for being too liberal with administrative salaries (Finsen and Finsen 1994, 83). Accepting a barely livable wage appears to be the sacrifice for doing service work with animals, and at times this was a feature of the work that was a source of pride for many employees. In this aspect, animal welfare work remains in keeping with the idea that it is a calling for which one is chosen, and not necessarily a chosen career. Unfortunately, it also meant that turnover at the shelter

Kelly Chapel brings in a stray dog.

was high, and less committed or more financially strapped people had to work two jobs or leave the field to seek higher wages.[4]

Several people, especially volunteers, often made large donations to local and national groups or helped specific animals out of their own pocket. Kelly Chapel works as a school teacher, but she spends a large amount of her own money to treat injured animals, to offer spays and neuters, to transport animals for people, and to house and foster them. Sometimes she even pays people to "buy" their puppies and kittens from them. Once her sister-in-law found a dog and called Kelly and asked her if she wanted to come and get it. After driving two hundred miles, Kelly arrived at 7:00 a.m. to pick up the stray. When her sister-in-law asked her if there was anything she wouldn't do for a dog, she replied, "I'd drive to the ends of the Earth for a dog!" (1999). Other volunteers have donated money to treat injured animals or assist with spay/neuter programs.

It has long struck me as curious why such a highly stressful, dangerous industry would pay its workers, including administrators, so horrendously. Apart from the obvious pay discrepancies between profit and not-for-profit work, when I asked the executive director why the pay was so low in shelters, he explained that traditionally, shelter jobs are held by women who are supplementing a husband's income. In my head, I ran down the list of the women I knew who worked in the kennel at that time. Three were single with children. Two were single and childless. The three men who worked in the kennel at that time were making $6 or $7 an hour as the primary breadwinners for their families. I thought about the people working in the front office. Most were women, some were married, but most were not. Most of them supported themselves and/or their families on the salary they made. Obviously the economic environment had shifted, but service work had not caught up. Although this executive director and the shelter board claimed they were working towards strengthening staff retention and making an effort to significantly increase the wages of its workers, I have never felt that animal welfare workers have been fully compensated—either financially or in other ways—for the work they do. I would suggest that in addition to the continued devaluing of women's skilled labor, the combination of women, marginalized men, and animals in this case produces a doubly devalued occupation in our culture.

So what does a worker in a shelter do to earn her wages? A kennel worker cleans the kennel and assists with processing animals. This entails several hours of scooping feces, feeding, disinfecting areas, washing linens and dishes, and checking the animals for signs of illness. Animals are selected, held and injected for euthanasia. This work also involves bathing animals and picking off ticks, handling lice and mange, being bled on, pooped on, peed on, possibly bitten, definitely scratched, and, what most would agree is the worst, cleaning up parvovirus-infected diarrhea. This is not a glorious job and not one for people with delicate sensibilities. A kennel worker has to maintain the gastric strength to clean up messes and the emotional sensitivity to kill animals with kindness.

Dealing with customers, in my opinion, is as stressful, and at times more so, than performing euthanasia. For one thing, customer service is extended throughout the entire workday, while killing occurs usually in the space of a couple of hours on an average day. Additionally, workers in the euthanasia room can still express their emotions in most cases, while front desk workers are required to mask their feelings for the public. Almost all kennel workers I interviewed told me that they could not work up front because they would kill somebody or get fired for saying something mean. The stress of dealing with difficult customers was not easy to dispel either, because immediately after that customer was handled, the worker was required to serve the next caller or customer. Susan Brannock told me that this was probably the one part of her job she would most like to see changed. She would like to have a mental health break after an upsetting experience occurs, but given the high volume of work in this position, there is usually no one available to relieve her.

Barbara Tellier explained to me that dealing with the public was the most difficult part of her job as well, especially in highly tense instances of cruelty investigations. She tries to be sure that any volunteer in her organization is accompanied by another volunteer during an investigation. She tries to be as polite as possible, but this isn't always possible, especially when the people she is investigating threaten her. Threats are another common feature of this work. Disgruntled customers have been heard to threaten not only the workers, but the animals as well. Barbara Tellier has somewhat of a reputation among the welfare community as being "difficult," but, as one of her own volunteers stated, "You know, Barbara is not the most cordial, but you know what? If I had been in this as long as she has, and seen as much stuff as she has, I might be like that too."

What I have found is that Barbara is often curt and terse—a result of being on a tight schedule and unwilling to engage in small talk. When I sat down to interview her on this subject, she confessed to being somewhat introverted. However, when it comes to the work she does, she can do a speech for forty-five minutes; she feels that strongly about it. What seemed to her to be common sense was in short order where she found neglected and abused animals. "[Animals] don't have to be pampered, but take care of them!"

Many workers commented on the "shyness" aspect of being involved in animal welfare. "I'm not a particularly social person. I've noticed that about the people around here. Most of them . . . would prefer not to have to interact with society. I think that's a common trend, we don't like people to begin with and we choose to surround ourselves with other people that we care about" (Hall). Another kennel worker told me that she was working there to make a difference to animals; "I don't really consider the people" (Walaski 1999).

A front office worker also takes the chance of being defecated and urinated on, bitten, scratched, and, in addition, yelled at by angry customers. The phone rings some days constantly, while the lobby is full of barking dogs, and cats crying in carriers. Because of the proximity to the administrative staff, the front office workers are more available to upper management to vent their frustrations. And if technology does not cooperate, the staff can be stuck trying to assist the public with frozen computer screens. One of the greatest hazards for front office workers is having their efforts sabotaged by management when a disgruntled customer decides to take their case to an administrator. More often than not, managers tend to side with the customer out of a sense of protecting public image, and not the individual animal in question. I have seen customers go through three female workers to find a way to circumvent policies, only to see the male manager publicly acquiesce to the customer and humiliate the workers in front of the people involved. In some cases, outsiders with prominence in the media intervened on behalf of irate customers, and, once again, in order to protect image and the source of funding, management placed animals in precarious positions in order to please one disgruntled customer.

Neither position—front office or processing—can be considered particularly free of hazard. Add to that the stress of becoming attached to animals only to see them die a week later, of seeing pets returned because the adopters thought that shelter dogs would already be housebroken, and of having to deny customers adoptions because they do not meet the shelter criteria. These jobs are not for the weak-willed or less convicted. Conviction, and not monetary reward, is obviously what keeps some of these workers in these positions for years.

Members of other groups also affirmed that most of their volunteers were women (Long 1999). According to Charles Peek et al., 80 percent of the workers and volunteers in animal rights and welfare are women. Some researchers have suggested that women are drawn to the field because they are socialized towards pursuing "caring and feeling occupations." Peek et al. suggest another approach to studying gender in shelters, one that corresponds to historical approaches such as Coral Lansbury's look at women and the vivisection movement. A structural approach takes into consideration women and their social location and relation to "hierarchical domination" (Peek, et al. 1996, 466). Although the results of their questionnaire do not guarantee this, it does suggest that future research might explore this possibility.

> Finally, other reactions of women to the experience of patriarchal oppression may increase their support for animal rights. One such reaction may be empathy with beings perceived as undergoing similar oppression. If one has experienced oppression, it does not necessarily take egalitarian ideology to heighten both awareness of and concern for others encountering similar ordeals. Our findings that both women and men lower in socioeconomic and age structures are more likely to affirm animal rights on one or both measures are consistent with this interpretation. (Peek, et al. 1996, 474)

Similarly, people who are accustomed to performing devalued labor, such as rearing children, service work, and housework, might also be able to relate to being a tossed-away pet (even if the pet originally cost several hundred dollars). Many of the people I met in this line of work had experienced other forms of interpersonal and institutional oppression. In simply talking to people in this line of work, one might not have an immediate sense that the workers had any personal experiences with suffering. Learning those types of secrets about people cannot always be accessed with a questionnaire or tape-recorded interview. However, as a peer and a friend to several of these workers, I learned that many of these individuals came from homes where they had been abused and turned out. Many of the women had been in marriages that involved sexual, physical, and emotional abuse. Some of the workers had cared for mentally and physically ill family members, or relatives with addictions. Some had lost loved ones in tragic accidents.

When I learned the personal stories of my co-workers and peers, I started to develop a theory (which unfortunately is not testable) that people are drawn to this work *because they can identify with the animals, and they can exert some control over suffering.* They are able to rescue them, care for them, and sometimes kill them because they identify with feelings of abandonment and have themselves been mistreated by people they trusted. In other words, there are times when death is not only the best alternative for the people involved, it is the only alternative. Perhaps, rather than see another cat in my life suffer from a horrible car accident, I was able to euthanize as a means of control over suffering. Watching my loved ones (human and animal) suffer in my childhood certainly gave me an overriding need to arrange strict control over my life as an adult.

These experiences are not confined to one gender. Several of the men I interviewed for this book mentioned instances of abuse from their own childhoods. None of these men came from wealth or even privilege, although there are certainly people with family wealth involved in animal welfare. Wealth does not spare people from emotional or physical cruelty and neglect. What differentiates many of these individuals, in my observation, is that they can relate to the abandoned dog in the kennel. They possess a compassion that derives from experience—compassion that develops from an experience of "oppression." Based on my observations and interviews, women *and* marginalized men may possess a more intense empathy for the suffering of animals. Rather than see these animals returned to a life of misery and entrapment, these workers would rather release them from physical torment and emotional neglect. They had a clear opinion of what a healthy family was, and they intended to provide these animals with the means to achieve that, or with a peaceful death. For those groups that did not advocate euthanasia, the only alternative to an adoptive family was life in a refuge (i.e., orphanage) or foster home.

When I mentioned my theory to Thelma Evans, she responded,

> I wouldn't argue that with you. I was trying to figure myself, when it came to actual suffering. Other than being hungry—I was in the last year of high school . . . The Crash of '29. My father lost his job and it was a good job and we lost the house and the whole family scattered and we were never together as a family again. And I went through agony trying to find a job, trying to eat. It would have been so much easier to be a prostitute, at least I would have had good food and a bed. But once things turned for me, I certainly have no complaint because I did nothing but go up. . . . I worked because I knew what was required. I didn't quibble over five minutes, I came in early and stayed late. (Evans 1999)

Thelma, therefore, committed herself later in life to seeking an ideal family for abandoned pets, thereby reconstructing her own life story through the lives of these animals. Starvation and suffering were not options.

On the level that euthanasia is an immediate answer to very real suffering, in the worldview of those performing it, it is an act of caring. The fact that a worker is forced to commit a killing in order to express caring is, as Arluke suggests, a paradox that is systematically and institutionally harmful (1996). But as Newkirk states, "Real life is full of nasty decisions that critics, philosophers, and fiddlers do not have to make" (Newkirk 1991, 1). I would also add that in some cases, death is the decisive gift that these workers are honored to provide for others because it was never an option for them.

As I mentioned in the previous chapter, euthanasia is the one activity that differentiates traditional shelter workers from the rest of the welfare community. It is the activity that draws lines within the traditional shelter between workers in different departments and between workers and volunteers. While in some ways it isolates the members of staff that perform this duty, it also creates for them a sense of cohesion and collective purpose (Arluke and Sanders 1996, 96–99). When Thelma and Ed decided to perform euthanasia at the Animal Humane Association, they lost some of their primary board members. Nonetheless, Thelma still believes her decision was sound and reasonable. Barbara Tellier supports euthanasia as a practical alternative to overpopulation as well, even though she does not personally perform euthanasia. Having grown up on a farm, she explained that her philosophy was that animals are meant to be "used, but not abused." This welfarist motto is a clear differentiation from animal rights advocates, and it fits quite nicely into the blurred category of pet-hood that these animals occupy.

Workers who had been in the field for a long period of time had experiences with various forms of humane killing. Thelma delivered animals to the pound for destruction in the chamber, prior to that facility switching its technique to lethal injection. Joel Warner, with about thirty years of experience in the welfare field, has also experienced a variety of killing methods. When he began the work in the 1960s, methods such as decompression and electrocution were being phased out of shelters in exchange for the more acceptable forms of injection. I have had an informal conversation with a worker who took a job as an animal control officer in a rural Texas town. Her supervisor tried to train her to destroy kittens by holding them in a bag up to the exhaust pipe of the truck. She opposed this and took it upon herself to learn how to inject.

As Arluke mentions, there are several layers of understanding to the experience of killing animals in shelters. On one level, workers strive towards developing a technical skill that provides comfort and ease for the animals (1996, 89). When one worker left the shelter after several years of working there, many people remarked that the employees *and* the animals would miss her skill as a "good shot." However, it was also recognized that having a technical skill was not as important as maintaining the emotional skills required to do this job daily. As Joel Warner stated, "I've never had anybody told [*sic*] me they enjoyed euthanasia. A lot of us that have been doing it a long time, we get hard core and we know it's something that we have to do but at the same time we also know that after years of experiencing it, we have to get out" (Warner 1997). The same worker who was once called "a good shot" told me later that she hoped she would never again have to kill an animal without good reason (i.e., health or injury). She admitted that until she "got out," she had been unaware of how performing euthanasia on a daily basis for so many years had affected her (Husler personal communication).

Sindy Tanner explained to me that she never saw herself in the position she was in at the shelter. "When I was a kid I used to think that some horrible man just went out there and killed them. . . . I never would have thought I was going to be the one to kill them. Never. I was the kind of girl that would go the pound and cry when I came out." I interviewed Sindy on her last day of work, and she told me that after thirteen years of killing animals, she was still attached to animals ("I'd like to say I've killed my last animal") but not particularly fond of people. Several workers conveyed their opinion that euthanasia should be available to people for medical and behavioral reasons as well (Husler 1997; Warner 1997). One worker stated, "If I could go like that, I'd be happy."

Workers stated that they managed the stress of this duty by increasing attention to their own pets, fostering animals, or focusing on the next animal walking in through the door. Even front office workers, though typically not involved in the actual practice of euthanasia, felt as if they were part of the process. It was a point of friction between those who actually performed the activity and those who did not, but as Susan states, this was not necessarily a clear division.

> I feel when I take an animal in, when I say it's all right for this animal to come here, even though I know this, this, and this, and I know it's probably not going to be adopted or whatever, or whatever the circumstances happen to be, I feel a responsibility for that animal while it's here and what the outcome is. And I'm not sure I would feel any more responsible if I feel the syringe, the needle inserted, and euthanized it myself. I don't know because I haven't been given the opportunity to find out. But I really don't think I would feel any differently if I did the physical euthanasia myself. . . . I'm involved. And I accept that responsibility. I don't shove it off on somebody else or pretend it's not there. . . . I'm not a person that thinks life at all costs. I think that death is very often a more suitable result than other options. (Brannock 1999)

Through several years of trying to understand my personal feelings about killing animals, I came to understand it by tracing the process of my incorporation into the shelter community. I approached this in a very conscious, self-reflexive way, because I was not only an employee of the shelter, I was also a researcher. "Going native" involved being constantly aware of the process of learning, conscious about how it compromised or added to my research, and concerned with how it affected my relationships with my co-workers. Just like many other workers, I accepted the job with the knowledge that animals were killed on a daily basis, but was not quite prepared for my reaction to actually seeing them be killed. I remember feeling somewhat nauseous and nervous about it, but also I felt a sense of morbid fascination for how it was done and for the presence of death.

Perhaps this flirtation with death is what led me to focus on euthanasia for so many years—it obviously related to my own issues over mortality and the place of suffering and animals in my spiritual belief system. To the surprise and suspicion of some of my co-workers, I volunteered to assist with euthanasia so that I could learn more about it (I was a front office worker, and was not required to perform it as part of my job). My original plan had been to expand Arluke's research. I had brought in an earlier version of his shelter article for a co-worker to read and had been surprised when she responded to it by saying, "He makes us sound like we're all brainwashed!" Instead of finding comfort in the universals, she was disturbed that he suggested she might have been unconsciously indoctrinated. This particular co-worker was the one who not only performed most of the euthanasia, she was the one who typically chose which animals would go. Without a doubt, she had the most stressful job in the entire facility. Were we, as shelter workers, simply duped into believing that euthanasia was necessary, or did we manage our justifications on more complex, personal, and emotional levels? What about our own experiences before we became "indoctrinated?" Through the process of friendship and peership, I discovered that there were clear parallels between my co-workers' past lives and the past lives of the animals we cared for. I also felt compassion for these animals based on my own experiences with loss, isolation and betrayal. I know that the other workers felt the same.

I spent the next three years writing about her response to Arluke's article, trying to defend my own observations and understand my relationship to killing. I will admit, and agree with Arluke, that once a worker has become a "dog killer," it gives him or her a sense of moral superiority and sets that person apart from the rest of the community. As one worker told me, if you love them—really love them—you have to be willing to do anything for them. Clean up after them and kill them (Tanner 1999). Killing animals implies that you are neither a "prissy girl, or a macho guy." Of course, I have seen plenty of macho guys and tough-looking women cry unabashedly over animal death or loss, even during generalized, abstract discussions. The point is, as Arluke suggests, performing euthanasia creates a collective and binding sense of belonging for the people that do it. The typical reply to the statement "How can you kill them? I just love animals too much," is answered by the reply "I love them enough to kill them."

I know that I did love many of the animals I helped to kill. My heart physically ached when I felt their bodies go limp in my arms. I was touched and moved by certain animals, specifically things I recall noticing about them as we were killing them, regardless of whether or not I recall their names. Having only performed euthanasia occasionally (and only as a holder), I can still remember certain deaths with clarity and tenderness. I was glad it was me that was there to hold them, because I knew I cared, and I would be able to remember them in my writing and in my heart.

My feelings about killing animals shifted some when I coordinated a camp for children in the summer of 1999. This camp brought together shelter dogs and children from foster families. Several of these children were medicated for anger and depression, as they had lived through experiences painful enough to strongly affect their behavior. About half of them came from treatment centers, the other half were recruited from the general community. The level of empathy between these two sets of "surplus" populations—shelter dogs and foster children—was astounding and it took me by surprise. With these children, I would be able to test my theory that suffering created a language between shelter animals and the people who cared for them.

I explained what euthanasia was to the ten-, eleven- and twelve-year-olds on the first day of camp. They understood it. They accepted my explanation for it. One child even answered my question of "OK, now what is euthanasia?" by replying "Children in China?" Bright kids! However, as the three weeks went by and the children came in every day to work with the dog they had been assigned to, they started noticing that certain dogs were no longer in the kennel. When they asked me what happened to the dogs, I replied honestly. "I don't know, and I would rather not find out." I was trying to gently remind them of the rules—that is, if the truth is going to hurt too much, then don't ask. This was a lesson every volunteer learned, and I was trying to teach the kids the lesson as well.

My carefully orchestrated avoidance tactic didn't do a great deal of good one day when a kennel worker walked out of the kennel with a dog named Shadow who was not chosen by the campers to be in camp, but with whom they were all familiar. I was not present, and so the details are based on hearsay, but from my understanding of the events, a child asked the worker where he was taking the dog. He replied, using the "motto" his supervisor had trained him to use, "He's going to be euthanized."

A frantic junior counselor summoned me back to the group to tell me there were kids in tears because Shadow was being euthanized. I gathered them around and reminded them that this was inevitable, and that I had thought they understood why it had to happen. Inside I was thinking of all the ways I could punish the guy who told them where he was taking Shadow, because I had instructed the kennel workers to have the euthanasia done before the children arrived or at least refer these issues to me first. The kids understood all of the rhetoric. They knew that they needed to spay and neuter. They knew that a commitment to a dog should be a lifetime one. The concepts were not difficult to deal with. What was hard about this was that *it hurt!*

I heard a voice ask, "Tami, can we say goodbye to Shadow?" I turned and smiled at the youngest camper, a nine-year-old who at that moment seemed more mature than any of us. "Of course." I brought Shadow from the holding cage and led him out for the children to pet and hug. He jumped all over them, oblivious to what was about to happen to him, but somewhat concerned that these kids were crying.

One child came running up then and asked me where Shadow was going. She was an extremely troubled child, in foster care, and she was also was my favorite. I told her he was going to be euthanized. I could see her trying to process this information and I could see how much work it was taking to do it. I put my hands on her shoulders, and I told her, "Listen, you know that only dogs and cats are euthanized when they're not adopted, right? Not little girls! Little girls and boys are not cats and dogs!" It turns out that she had taken my rhetoric much further and identified with homeless animals to the point of believing that children who weren't adopted could also be killed. Her treatment coordinator told me that it wasn't until a few weeks after camp ended and the child's medication was finally regulated that she understood that only dogs and cats were killed for not being adopted. In my opinion, this child proved my theory.

After each child who wanted to said goodbye, I walked Shadow back to his cage. I looked down at him as I slid the leash off his neck and ran my fingers through his thick Aussie fur. He was charcoal and black, a big bear of a dog, and he was obviously a dope with a big sweet heart. Right then I broke down and cried, for the first time in years (over euthanasia). I apologized to him. I took a couple of breaths, wiped my face on my sleeve, and went back to the kids. The shift had occurred because I saw him as those children saw him—powerless, victimized, tossed away—just as many of them had become, just as many of them felt every day of their lives. I realized how truly powerless I was when I reconnected with the little girl I once was. I couldn't keep any of them from suffering. After that hard summer, the same summer when I put down Camille, it took me a very long time to walk back to the processing building when I knew they were killing. Not one single motto or justification could compensate for the pain in my heart and gut when I thought about those animals dying, especially animals that had briefly known so much love and attention—some for only four days or three weeks, and one in particular for five years. It wasn't that I was upset about how they died. I mourned for the potential lost. I felt guilty for showing them, if only briefly, how life could be. I felt exceptionally saddened for thinking I had the power to make their lives any different. I was overwhelmed and, by most commonly understood definitions, I was experiencing the beginning effects of burn-out.

Putting down a personal pet usually produces conflict for workers. For one thing, they sometimes feel like they should either perform the euthanasia or be present. When I interviewed Paula about euthanasia, she had just put her dog down the week before. She explained that she had always managed to maintain some distance from the animals, but this didn't make the job any easier. Her real desire was to make people realize what they were doing when they relinquished animals to shelters.

This brief statement also illustrates the fragile boundaries workers draw between themselves, other workers, personal pets and shelter animals, and the public.

> One thing I do think, and this is to the euthanasia, is as long as I've been doing it, and I did a lot of it, and I said that the reasons why I kept. . . . I was able to separate. When I had to put Stinky down, they asked me if I wanted to be there. And I had no other thought in my mind. I mean, I knew I couldn't inject, but I knew I could hold her and be with her. And I just wish people would be with them when they go because it's hard now and people need to witness that. . . . I don't think that's something that you can make people do because if I wasn't used to it I don't know how well I would be. I think I'm doing OK. . . . I'm not doing great. . . . I can understand not wanting to force somebody to see that. I surely wouldn't want to force a child to have to see that. (Golden 1999)

Some shelters have televised euthanasia in an effort to increase adoptions and funding. Several years ago, Animal Humane posted a billboard that simply stated, "Stop us before we kill again." There is a fine line that is drawn here. As Susan Brannock said,

> Any shelter has . . . a black cloud that hangs over it. Part of that's
> like the Disney Syndrome from *Lady and the Tramp* and other
> movies that the dog catcher or the animal shelter is like the
> most evil place—the bad guy's the dog catcher. Shelters haven't
> been given a very good reputation by Hollywood . . . but from
> the responses of the people that bring animals here . . . and peo-
> ple that come to adopt, most people think that AHA is really
> doing a pretty good job and has a lot of heart. (Brannock 1999)

How do other shelter workers manage the stress of their jobs? I
received a great assortment of answers to this question. A few workers mentioned managing stress with the use of alcohol and marijuana. Almost all
of the people who relayed this information to me claimed that they
smoked or drank after work, but I have observed workers occasionally
drinking or smoking during a workday. Luckily this occurred very infrequently, maybe only two or three times in the four years I have been
involved. Four years ago, when it was suggested by upper management
that drug testing be part of the job requirement, it was countered by middle management that "half of the staff" would fail the test.

The executive director explained to me that in his experience,
which spanned thirty years in the field, it was common for workers to manage job-related stress in unhealthy ways, including alcohol, drugs, violence,
and in more extreme cases, suicide. One of the first stories Joel told me was
how he was introduced to shelter work in the first place. After being convinced to enter into the shelter field by his personal veterinarian, Dr. Roth,
on his first day at work he helped him put down eighty-five animals. When
they finished this grisly job at 11:30 p.m., Joel went home and Dr. Roth
stayed to finish the paperwork. At 4:00 in the morning, Joel received a
phone call from the morning kennel worker, who told him to come to the
shelter quickly because there was a problem with Dr. Roth. When Joel
arrived, he found the veterinarian sitting in a chair, dead, with an IV in each
arm. "That was my introduction to euthanasia." Not only had he lost his
peer and veterinarian, he had lost a friend as well (Warner 1997).

Obviously, smoking pot might offer a more effective way to deal
with stress than suicide, but there were other ways (legal ways) workers and
volunteers managed stress as well. About half of the kennel workers
smoked cigarettes, and smoking was a deeply entrenched part of the work
routine. Joel told me that during smoke breaks on euthanasia days, the
staff at one shelter he worked in would step outside and holler after per-

forming euthanasia—holler at the top of their lungs until they felt a little better. Talking to other people about it was a way many people managed the stress of their jobs, and even though many workers had family members who could not personally do shelter work, they were happy to offer emotional support to their loved ones.

I interviewed Julie Lorrin during her last week at the shelter, where she had been an employee for eleven years. The stress of years of killing animals, staff upheaval, interpersonal politics, and the feelings of loss when a precious animal was not adopted led her to decide to go back to school. As she said, "That way, I don't have to kill anything again. . . . I've had my fill of getting attached to things for them to be put to sleep." Although she wasn't as interested in working with computers as she was with cats, she was willing to make the trade-off. She worked in the cat room. I asked her if she had ever not been able to become attached to the cats she cared for, and she replied, "Oh yeah, you'd think that it would stop. You'd think that after so long, it would stop, but it doesn't ever stop. . . . I generally become so close to the cats that are like, so afraid, you know? I can get them to come out of their shell just in time for them to be euthanized, you know? That really breaks my heart" (Lorrin 1999).

Julie was able to recognize that her time to leave this line of work had finally arrived. But sadly, other workers do not always pay attention to signals that suggest that they have reached the boiling point. I have seen some workers unable to manage the stress of daily operations to the point where they were fired. Although the shelter does not make counseling available to the workers, some of them have attended seminars and retreats aimed at reducing stress and offering guidelines for the effective management of stress. Workers have reported to me that they have had nightmares about euthanasia, including ones where they woke up in the freezer, came to work to find animals hanging from meat hooks, and one worker had a dream that everywhere he went, no dog would stop and talk to him. They all ran from him, as if they knew who he was and what he did (Andes personal communication).

Sick humor was another way workers managed their stress. It was also a means by which subgroups of workers compartmentalized others in relation to their work. If volunteers were privy to the jokes that surrounded euthanasia, it was highly uncommon, because this was an activity that was reserved for the staff that performed the job. One worker told me variants on every dead baby joke he had ever heard, but substituted the word "puppy" for baby. This made it seem even more gruesome considering the work we were actually doing, and the fact that puppies did pile up in ways that might require the imagined use of a pitch fork to clear them out (McNutt personal communication).

Workers have reported playing puppet with the bodies of kittens, or cracking jokes about decapitations for rabies testing, which was one of the most gruesome jobs they were required to perform. When I asked these workers about the use of black humor, several responded by stating, "If we didn't laugh about it, all we'd do is cry." However, I would like to mention that sick humor was not always used in appropriate situations. New or inexperienced workers who were not properly acculturated were often chastised for performing the jokes in front of outsiders. And some seasoned workers still did not apply humor to an extremely stressful, intimate activity.

Although these workers put in forty hours a week or more, work-related stress is not limited to actual employees of the shelter. The volunteers at this shelter and the persons I interviewed who work with no-kill or cruelty investigative groups also manage a high level of stress in their positions. Volunteers became visibly stressed during disease outbreaks, especially foster volunteers who might have foster animals up for adoption in the kennel or cat room. Beth Petronis explained to me that although she doesn't really experience stress from her volunteer obligations, she does get "sad." The idealism she had when she first came to work at the shelter had been somewhat readjusted by a number of experiences over three years of volunteering. As she told me, when she started working there, she thought she could "save every one," and that seeing animals "with a lot of potential" be euthanized confused and upset her (Petronis 1999). Nearly every volunteer and most of the employees I have worked with, and this would probably be a figure somewhere in the hundreds, have had a hard time rationalizing euthanasia at some point or another. Many continue to work in the shelter, despite being ethically opposed to the practice in the first place. I got some interesting insight on this phenomenon from Jane Long, the volunteer and board member of PACA, a no-kill group. I asked her how she felt about people "switching teams" and working for more than one group. She said, "Some people can't work in a traditional shelter knowing that those animals aren't going to be there tomorrow because they're going to be euthanized. I couldn't. I couldn't. Some people will volunteer there because they view our animals as already saved, which is true. That's a truism as well" (Long 1999).

Unfortunately, if these issues over euthanasia are not at some point resolved, volunteers either stop coming in or come in and complain to staff when animals "disappear" from the kennel. As Sindy Tanner explained, this pressure from a group of three hundred well-intentioned strangers does nothing to alleviate the guilt the staff feels over their jobs. Little do they know that she would some nights go home and cry from the blame she felt from the volunteers. " 'You did it.' Well, it wasn't like I chose to do it. Somebody had to do it or it was going to just continue, on and on" (Tanner 1999).

One of the benefits in working for a large organization such as AHANM is that it can support a large, diverse staff of volunteers. This was not the case in other shelters I visited, and it showed, because there was no self-policing in those other shelters. While some volunteers took their criticisms to extremes and actually drove deep wedges between staff and volunteers, some were able to apply their commitment to animals to a healthy realism and were a great help to staff. When workers complained about volunteers, I would explain that on a functional level, they are invaluable to an organization that deals with issues of cruelty and kindness. Volunteers often serve as a buffer between front office staff and the public, offering their distance in place of the tension created by difficult circumstances. Volunteers also keep workers in sight of the details and triumphs—which are easy to lose when workers are confronted daily with a large volume of animals. A shelter that does not appreciate the functional role of volunteer staffs will undoubtedly encounter great difficulty voicing their philosophies to the general community. As a voice for the shelter and especially as an advocate for the animals, volunteers are crucial to a successful animal shelter.

There are difficulties and challenges interacting with the public and co-workers, dealing with other groups with differing philosophies, and trying to negotiate a manageable emotional position within the shelter culture. The relationships that keep workers and volunteers returning to the work are the ones they maintain with the animals. When Sindy left her job, she worried that no one else would adequately take care of the dogs. "Who's going to make sure the old dogs have their canned food, you know? That they have warm beds, that they're not all wet?" (Tanner 1999). Julie also mentioned that she would miss taking care of the shy and scared cats (Lorrin 1999). At Thanksgiving dinner, Barbara Tellier gave each of her guests an unsocialized kitten to handle, and throughout the evening played "musical kittens" so the animals would get used to being handled. She worries that when she finally retires, no one will take over her organization or her duties, and that horses in the state will once again have no one on their side (Tellier 1999).

Two of the volunteers I included in my interviews were Beth Petronis and Sylvia Taborelli, each of whom donates time and money to various causes at the shelter. The most impressive attribute these two women contribute to our daily work, though, is focus and commitment. Neither allows small details to elude her, despite the frantic pace of an average workday. Both maintain a sense of humor, justice, and respect for the people who are trying to make an honest living in this field, and both are truly interested in helping people and animals. In summation, they possess the characteristics that make up the very best in animal welfare volunteers. One area that both Sylvia and Beth commit themselves to is increasing the effectiveness of Animal Humane's lost and found service. Beth has traced dogs across the country for owners. Each of them applies her professional skills to the jobs she does at the shelter, as well as a healthy dose of compassion. The following example illustrates this.

> I went back to processing. There was already a sign on her cage to "Hold Min," which is hold minimum and that really perplexed me. In talking with processing folks they decided she was head shy and a fear biter. So I went in her cage and I was just talking to her and she was a great dog until I would go to pet her from the top down and it seemed to me that there was something unusual about this dog . . . it wasn't just a behavioral problem. I talked to Tracy and found the status . . . this was a tag that couldn't be traced but I really felt that there was something strange about this animal's behavior, something inconsistent. I remember saying to Tracy, "I think the dog is saying she's in pain." Because it's just not normal. And that there was something that she was telling us, that we should be careful, "Don't touch me there." It turned out . . . the owner did finally come forward and claim the dog, and it turned out that this dog had fallen off a truck when she was younger and had broken her neck and her back. And she was terribly afraid of people touching her there. So, while this dog probably could have been destroyed because she was aggressive and they might have said . . . she was a danger to the staff . . . she was speaking . . . and it just took somebody to give the time to think about her. So she did go home. And one of the clues I had . . . the owner worked for a chiropractor and I thought, oh gosh, I'll bet this person took this dog in for chiropractic treatment. And she said . . . that had been the case and that had made the problem worse. (Petronis 1999).

This, I believe, is the crucial difference between full-time workers and volunteers who spend anywhere from three to twelve hours a week in the shelter or on rescue work in general. Workers see the volume of the overpopulation problem, in addition to trying to become acquainted with each and every animal that walks through the door. For every purebred cocker spaniel, ten rottweiler mix puppies will be admitted. And for every Siamese cross there will be twenty nondescript black kittens needing medical attention and foster homes. This is an impossible situation, and as Sindy says, it continues "on and on." Volunteers have the opportunity to listen to specific animals in those cases when workers cannot.

Abuse cases sometimes made the day-to-day stress nearly unbearable as well, and moved the workers to anger and disgust. The following two stories illustrate how some aspects of this work test the limits of faith in humanity, and provide workers in this field with limited alternatives.

> The worst one I can remember, I came across this matted, dirty, chained up little poodle thing. I couldn't get near it to pick it up physically, so I just got it by the chain and drug it all the way into the clinic. When we got it, we anesthetized it and we found that her leg had been lacerated with wire all the way through to the bone. Through all the hair you couldn't see that. She was totally emaciated . . . they had amputated her leg . . . the pelt they got off her was as big as she was. Just disgusting! Poor thing. (Tanner 1999)

Cynthia Baca's most memorable animal suggests that even within the shelter system, some animals and workers are not always heard when they are obviously speaking to those who are in positions to help.

> The animal I remember most from the entire year I've been here was when I first started, and she's a cat named Sunshine. Sunshine was at Eubank [a satellite adoption clinic] . . . for three months. . . . It was right before Halloween so we had to hold on to her because she was mostly black, she was black and white, and she was really scared. You'd open the cage and she'd cower in the corner, and we chalked that up to her being depressed or just being in the cage. And she was about four years old. And a few weeks went by and she still wouldn't come out of her litter box. We hardly ever had to clean it because she wouldn't eat. She was losing weight. And everybody worried about her. No one could take her out though because she'd slash us. And so

she was really scared. And it was just horrible, because after a month and a half we knew that anyone who would possibly want to adopt her had already seen her at Eubank because it's the same people coming in every week. And so we asked her to be sent back here or sent somewhere else and they sent her to Renaissance [another satellite] for a week. She didn't do well. The staff didn't want to deal with her there because she was nasty sometimes and I knew it was just because she was scared. And they brought her back here [to the main shelter] and she was in the cat room for a couple of weeks and then they sent her back to Eubank, which was a horrible mistake. And after three months of just being in this cage, they finally decided to put her down and it was because all of us got together and said, "You really need to do this. Nobody's adopting her. All of us want to take her home, but she hates other cats, she doesn't like dogs, she's not particularly nice with other people." You know, what can you do? (Baca 1999)

Individual acts of kindness, sometimes performed by the same "uncaring" public, can be reason enough to continue in the line of work. Though it is their job to liberate animals from oppressive situations, the network of kindred spirits performing the same work sustains many of the workers, and keeps an ember lit that fosters personal sacrifice and loss. Susan Brannock relayed the following story as illustrative of the kinds of instances she chooses to focus on, rather than the twenty difficult situations that happened before and after.

A woman called me right after a snowstorm . . . and her neighbors had left and left their pets. And the German shepherd mix had had puppies and they also had a wolf hybrid, a male. And the male wolf hybrid came to her door two or three times and she'd open the door, the dog would run off and she had no idea what was going on. He brought her one of the whelps. It was like he was trying to tell her, "We have new babies, help us!". . . She was crying as she was telling me and she was so obviously moved by this animal trying to get across to this stupid human, she said she thought animals only did that in Lassie movies. (Brannock 1999)

All of these are examples of moral stories in which people are obligated to help animals, and animals are, consciously or not, negotiating their own fate. The wolf hybrid seemingly solicited assistance from the woman caller, reinforcing the idea that pets are members of families, while Sunshine resisted incorporation by her rescuers up until the end. The poodle in the first story, though assisted by workers, had obviously been so neglected and possibly abused that it had to be anesthetized before people could get near it to help it. While workers can maintain a powerful amount of control over the lives of these animals (to the point of ending their lives), it is wrong to assume that the animals themselves have no real input in their own fates. As many of the stories in this chapter have shown, it was the individual animal—a personal pet, a rescued animal, a shelter mascot, an abuse case—that made an impact on these workers more than any other philosophy or ideal. These are real relationships that occur on a daily basis in animal welfare work. I was most convinced of this when I or other workers recognized animals that returned as strays to the shelter. Despite the multitude of animals received, employees could visually recall certain animals.

Preparing the animals for adoption is the main goal of both workers and volunteers in the shelter. When a worker or volunteer can convince a stranger of the special characteristics of a specific animal, when they achieve the goal of recognizing the personality of a pet and get other people to recognize it, their struggles are rewarded. Understanding the needs of a family, and which pet out of sixty will meet those needs, requires intimate knowledge of that specific animal. Although I have ceased placing animals in new homes, I have kept as reminders thank you notes and post-adoption photos of some of the animals I was personally responsible for successfully placing. Those successes do happen, and they happen frequently. They are the sweet reward for the workers and volunteers after the many false attempts and tragedies.

Some animals and adoptions become legends in shelter lore and through their stories affect the history of organizations. Some animals make a small difference to a select group of people. Quite often, the factors that allow these animals to survive the shelter and become members of families are a combination of the stories the workers construct about the animals and the actions or personalities of the animals themselves. In the next chapter, I will introduce you to a few of the shelter animals that made this work possible.

Bridging the Bond

"While it is obvious that animals are 'real' physical entities, their meaning to humans is socially constructed, reflecting the cultural concerns of those who think about them" (Arluke 1994, 143).

In different contexts, the same animal can have different meanings, or different meanings in the same contexts, and so on. In addition, as it relates to this work, the same animal can have different meanings over the course of his or her life. Some of these meanings rely on the learned or innate behavior of the animal, or on his appearance, but the meanings of the behavior and appearance are translated and codified by the people with whom he interacts. However the animal may be constructed by humans, he also plays an active part in that construction *if people are willing to allow for that voice.*

When attempting to provide care for shelter animals, the workers and volunteers naturally search for analogs in their own experience for how the animals feel when they are left in shelters or with foster families. Workers seldom analyze the theoretical implications of assuming a dog is lonely, depressed, in mourning, or scared. It is accepted that cats can be terrified, friendly, boisterous, or pissed off. This is one arena where anthropomorphism is highly relied upon by the caretakers of animals (Lockwood 1995, 192). As Randall Lockwood suggested, projective anthropomorphism is a tool that makes our lives as social creatures possible, and it is important for workers to be aware of how dogs and cats are adjusting to life in a shelter environment or a foster home. There are times, in play or jest, when workers extend some anthropomorphic traits to animals in order to codify their behavior or justify varieties of interactions, employing more extreme forms such as dressing an animal up for symbolic purposes or assuming that he is motivated by feelings of revenge or premeditated aggression. I don't think that most workers truly believe that the animal is behaving outside of its ability, but they do use these varieties of anthropomorphism in order to tell an entertaining and/or educational story. For instance, I have previously written about the characteristic of "tortitude," a trait associated with calico and tortoise-

A stray dog is admitted at AHANM

Photograph by the author

shell cats that can only be explained by defining it as a form of feline "premenstrual syndrome." This characterization of calicoes was a gendered association created by female workers who have to be careful when interacting with strange animals. Some authors have suggested that color in cats can determine some aspects of personality, especially since cats were bred for color more than size or shape (Ritvo 1986, 118). Most of the workers in the shelter will agree that *some* cats with these colors exhibit certain traits that are remarkably similar to those associated with PMS, such as irritability, fickleness, and short tempers. This is not the case, however, for *all* calico or tortoiseshell cats. It is a construction based on a combination of similar features between individual animals performed by a group of people who will understand the multilayered meanings of such an analogy.

The construction of an animal's personality also has several layers and relies on a variety of considerations. In keeping with the duality of my role as researcher and shelter worker, I will undoubtedly allow anthropomorphic language to guide many of the stories I will tell in this chapter. I will also draw material from interviews with workers and volunteers. Their desire to understand what an animal might be trying to communicate is the basis of the bonds that are temporarily established while animals are in transition between permanent homes. Ultimately, what I hope to suggest is that while workers construct narratives to set parameters around the work they do, animals in these environments are actors and may contribute towards their own fate. Consciousness is not the issue (in this inquiry)—the issue is that despite institutional training, despite cultural standards for how certain breeds or species behave, animals are still individuals, capable of acting independently (within the boundaries of their physiology) and without human determination. Although workers rely on socially created constructs to find new homes for or justify the deaths of these abandoned pets, they also rely on the behaviors of the animals to decide their fates, even if the animals are not conscious of the potential outcome. Despite the control shelter workers have over these animals, the animals themselves have motivations, desires, expressions, and needs. Workers take these, translate them, and then take other socially constructed messages into consideration when determining the fate of the animal. Just as the institution of sheltering animals does not necessarily override how the workers experience them, neither do the workers consistently neglect the individuality of their nonhuman clients.

I will begin by discussing a few cases where animals have lost their individual personalities in the process of becoming constructed by shelter personnel. The animals I have chosen to represent in these cases are ones that were involved in a narrative that had a lasting impact on the organizations involved, but less for *who* they were than for what happened to them. Following their stories, I will trace the average experience of an animal in the traditional shelter, as it goes from a nameless stray to a codified individual. These animals have a wide variety of experiences, as this section will show. Finally, I will discuss those animals that

Photographs by the author

A Labrador cross assumes the "pity position." His behavior, expression, breed, and coloring would be considered highly adoptable.

A dalmatian exhibits traits that do not promote his possible adoption. His adoptability would be considered low, a combination of his breed, age, and high activity level. These dogs were relinquished to shelters in high volume following the release of popular children's movies. The media covered this event to the extent that they portrayed the breed as difficult to train and unmanageable. Now they have a more difficult time being placed from shelters. This is a case, similar to the portrayals of pit bulls, where the news media sensationalized a breed literally to death.

resist codification in the shelter environment, particularly those who do not fit neatly into the stereotypical image of "family member" or "victim/shelter pet" because they have the perceived ability to hurt people or other animals. Rather than being sentimentalized, dogs such as pit bulls and rottweilers may have a more difficult time being processed by a shelter because the construction of how they are perceived can overpower their individuality. At the same time it is their individuality among other pets that makes them resist the same cultural construction. I will use these cases to show how cultural construction functions on different levels and provides for a variety of social expectations.

This chapter will show how workers translate the needs and desires of animals in order to maintain the bond until another permanent home is found. And in some cases it will show how that bond is severed through the death of the animal. It will also present the degrees to which I can adequately reconstruct these images of animal personality as an ethnographer. It will be obvious to the reader which animals I knew personally and which animals were strangers to me, and how the method of objective ethnography can offer only so much in terms of personal knowledge to its readers. As an ethnographer and a writer, I am part of that process of cultural construction, just as I played a part (or not) in the lives of these animals. I will begin with an animal who has become a legend within one group, an animal I've known only as a construct.

Sometimes there are individual animals that make a lasting impact on a group of people, on a movement, on a philosophy. The individual life of Koko, the gorilla who uses sign language, has had an incredible impact on our culture by reorganizing the boundaries between people and animals and the use of language as a dividing feature of that boundary. Koko has undoubtedly had a tremendous impact on everyone who has cared for her, handled her, or even exchanged some words with her (Haraway 1989, 143). She may have also had an impact on people, including researchers such as myself, who have never even met her. No animal, including a shelter animal, is completely independent of interactions with people. Even feral animals rely on our garbage and abandoned shelters, and they live in areas bound by the prescribed divisions of our communities, free spaces, and wilderness areas. In each of our personal lives, most of us can name at least one animal that has changed our awareness, or touched our lives with love, terror, or discovery.

Charlie Black did that for the Animal Humane Association and for the animal welfare community in Albuquerque. What happened to him as a puppy reinforced the ideals of the fledgling humane society in the late 1960s and early 1970s. It created a point of conflict between members of the group and of the community, and he provided the society with "a symbol of what we are trying to do," in the words of Colonel Evans (National Humane *Shoptalk*, January 1970; *Albuquerque Journal* 13 November 1969).

Charlie Black, mascot of the Animal Humane Association of New Mexico, Inc., 1969–1986.

Charlie's story was defined and articulated by national humane societies, by the two boys who abused him, by the family that originally rejected him, by the journalists who recounted his story, by the children who donated their pennies to his rehabilitation, and by the workers in the shelter who actually knew him. I am also participating in the (re)construction of his life by repeating his story within the pages of this book. His story was, as James Turner has suggested, one that echoed the morality of sympathy for suffering. Charlie's suffering and rehabilitation become a prototype for the stories the workers later tell to inspire sympathy for other shelter residents.

Charlie's story is especially timely as the cultural conversation revolves increasingly around the apparent assumed ease with which American children perform acts of cruelty against others. Humane societies have seized this cultural dialogue as a means by which to effect change and protect children, animals, and society from the threat of cruelty and violence. It is the same rhetoric that was employed in the nineteenth century in its desire to elevate the lower classes and save boys from lives of violence.

A visit to either the American Humane Association (AHA) or the Humane Society of the United States websites (www.americanhumane.org and www.hsus.org) will introduce a person to the "Link," as it is currently called by AHA, between violence to animals and violence to people. Significant studies have employed qualitative methods to *prove* that there is a link between animal abuse and violent behavior. Feminist authors have also pinpointed the link between animal abuse and domestic violence, and several shelters now provide safe haven for animals taken from abusive homes while human victims recover their independence (Adams 1994, 1994). The rhetoric in these pamphlets and informational brochures is the same rhetoric that social advocates employ to effect change. If we protect animals from cruelty, we will indirectly be protecting people. Therefore, the interests of people take center stage, and it is only by association that animals are protected. This has been a basic tenet in welfarist philosophy since the inception of the humane movement.

The "buzz word" in our culture, and in the subculture of animal welfare work, is *empathy*. The common definition used in the shelter environment is an ability to sense that another being has feelings, and to treat it accordingly. Empathy could be understood as *the communicative act* that transpires between two individuals who do not share a common verbal language, a form of the "projective anthropomorphism" that Randall Lockwood suggested that researchers use when studying animals (1995). People use it to help animals, and we in turn glorify a pet's ability to sense our feelings of sadness, loneliness, and joy. I have utilized this skill while performing fieldwork, and shelter workers come into the work with this skill already in their repertoire. Over time they refine it as they are trained and as they encounter new animals. It is the *lack of empathy* that many name as the cause of animal abuse and other forms of interpersonal violence.

Charlie Black's story illustrates and reconstructs the philosophy that animal abuse will lead to criminal behavior. The events that led to the construction of this rhetoric for AHANM—the experience of the puppy—are quickly overshadowed by what the events say about people—namely the two boys who committed the cruel act. This story is an example of how the cultural narrative nearly obliterates the individuality of the victim, and the victim becomes a symbol for a cause. Over time, especially since his death, Charlie has become an icon for the shelter—a link to the past and a reminder of the purpose and mission of the organization.

On February 12, 1969, two boys, one eight and one eleven (by most reports) were walking down a city street in downtown Albuquerque when a small black puppy started following them. Details of why the pup followed the boys are conflicting. The official document printed by AHANM described the boys as the owners of the pup. Some newspaper accounts claim that the dog belonged to the boys, but another article stated that the boys encountered a man who asked them to be on the lookout for a dog matching this description. When the boys found the dog and took it to the man, he then apparently changed his mind and told them he didn't want him anymore. When the boys left, the dog continued following them. First they tried telling it to leave, then threw rocks at him. Finally, they took the puppy to the fourth floor of a parking garage and threw him off the top.

Courtesy of AHANM

Photo of the parking garage where Charlie was "tossed" by the children.

The puppy survived the "toss" and suffered a fractured pelvis and two broken legs. Bystanders gathered to protect the puppy from cars, and the boys were caught and then arrested. One of the bystanders telephoned AHANM and asked them to assist with the pup. Thelma and Ed Evans called their veterinarian and asked her to treat him. The little dog stayed in the hospital for several weeks, and then went into foster care while his injuries healed further.

Class implications arise in several of the articles about Charlie Black, with benevolent charitable children situated in suburban neighborhoods, and the "juvenile delinquents" who committed the act residing in an urban section of the city. This rhetoric is still common in animal welfare circles in Albuquerque; most of the pet overpopulation and stray animal problems are assumed to originate in the ethnic and poor neighborhoods. The real danger to animals is from poor, uneducated peoples who fight them, use them for purposes other than companionship, or can't afford adequate veterinary care.

In one of the articles, the older boy is portrayed as being a mere bystander. Although he signs a statement saying that he helped the younger boy throw the dog off the roof, he later tells the judge it was an accident. He then says that while his friend dropped the dog and then ran, he stayed on the roof. When the judge asks the boy's parents what he had told them about it, they respond by stating that they hadn't even known he was involved in the case because he was living with his sister at the time. They found out he was involved only when they read about it in the newspaper (*Albuquerque Journal*, 15 April 1969). This rhetoric is similar to what we hear from the media regarding the breakdown of the traditional family and the subsequent tendencies of children from those homes. If there aren't parents available to monitor the activities of children, then those children will go astray. Both boys were sentenced to perform community service. Nothing further is known about their fates, or if they grew up to become more creative and violent criminals.

We do know what happened to Charlie Black. The interest in his story was great enough to raise several hundred dollars for his rehabilitation, and AHANM decided to adopt him and make him a shelter mascot. This decision received

Albuquerque children rally around Charlie.

some criticism from other members of the organization, who claimed that when the original owners tried to get Charlie back, the Evanses refused them. The critics accused the Evanses of setting the reclaim fees too high for the family, even though most of the money was actually donated by citizens (*Albuquerque Journal*, 15 March 1970).

In response to these accusations, Col. Evans explained that the family did not come forward to claim Charlie until five weeks after the accident occurred, despite efforts by AHANM to locate the original owners. When informed that there would be medical bills and further expenses for Charlie's care, the family decided to sign the dog over to the shelter. The article also mentions that one`veterinarian had suggested the dog be destroyed, but the community interest in his rehabilitation guaranteed his medical recovery (*Albuquerque Journal*, 15 March 1970).

Charlie not only went on to become the shelter mascot, he also received the Lassie Gold Award medal from the Campbell Soup Company. "The awards are given for any unusual act of canine behavior or human behavior on behalf of canines," stated the local television celebrity who nominated Charlie for the award (*Albuquerque Journal*, 13 November 1969). Merely through survival, Charlie became a hero. A hero for what he symbolized and solicited—the cruelty people inflict on animals, and the community outcry against such public acts of animal cruelty. His story was a perfect transmission for the humane moral agenda. Charlie was part of nearly every fund raising campaign carried out by AHANM over the course of the next sixteen years. Most notable of these was the Doggie Derby, an annual contest held for children and their pets in the community.

So what was Charlie like? According to Thelma, he was a character full of personality. When later members of the AHANM staff met

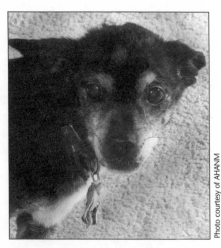

Photo courtesy of AHANM

One of the last photographs taken of Charlie, November 1986.

him, he was in his declining years and one person told me he was quite temperamental. Nonetheless, he was the visible evidence of AHANM's mission, he was a local victim turned hero, and he symbolized through his own "spunk," which is visible in the publicity photo, the purpose behind shelter work.

Other groups also had animals that created a controversy and became a means of soliciting community support for humane intervention. Barbara Tellier told me the story of Hank, a horse that received a great deal of media coverage for AAAA. Hank was found in a neighborhood associated with the upper classes with a garbage can as a water bucket—a bucket that Barbara claimed was usually turned over on its side when she would go to investigate the state of the horse. The story she told me was that the owner could not be convicted of animal abuse, despite the fact that he seemed to be starving the horse "in order to break him" (Tellier 1999). Barbara could not get assistance from any government agency to rescue the horse and so, for the first time since she began her rescue work, she was forced to hire an attorney. Eventually, after weeks of intensive work trying to get Hank away from his owner, Barbara was successful in delivering him from the neglect. A member of her organization adopted him. His story as it was covered in the media allowed for a great deal of coverage for AAAA and the work Barbara was trying to do (Tellier 1999).

Mascots serve an important function for humane societies. They provide workers with an animal to rally around and bond with. They present a recognizable image of concern and caring to the public, and their inspiring stories of tragedy and triumph often lead people to this work. They provide

workers with a recognizable, notable
story with which to inspire empathy
in others. Nonetheless, through the
use of these animals as symbols for
the work of the rescue groups, they
lose aspects of their individuality.
Workers retell stories of abuse, recov-
ery, and triumph, and in the process
some of the special characteristics of
the animal are lost. There are a number of graves for what I assume were

Photographs courtesy of A.A.A.A

ABOVE: A close up of Hank's torso.

BELOW: Hank, one year after the rescue.

mascot animals at AHANM, complete with gravestones, and none of the current workers seem to have any idea who the animals were. Few know the
details of Charlie's story, because his story has little to do with their daily interactions with living animals. The next section, based on interviews and direct
participant-observation, will illustrate how the staff at the traditional shelter
handles an average animal. Their experiences become only slightly differenti-
ated among the thousands of others voices in the shelter world.

The Daily Interactions

During my interviews, I asked workers to describe their role in the process
of recognizing the personalities of the animals that stay in the shelter. I
videotaped and photographed these various stages. I wanted to be sure I
had included as many details as possible from the experience of the animal. When I attended an adoption clinic with PACA, I videotaped the ken-

nel cards of several animals up for adoption, and asked volunteers to give me as much information as they could about them. This section will trace the process by which an animal designated as either someone's pet or a stray becomes defined as a shelter or rescue animal. During that process, certain animals have the ability to inspire different levels of familiarity with the workers, depending on their histories and personalities. Some of these strategies are successful and some are not.

At AHANM and the various rescue groups, people are encouraged to make appointments or reserve cages prior to bringing the animal in. PACA requires animals to be spayed or neutered and vaccinated, and owners can attend adoption clinics and place their own pets. If they wish to turn the animal over to PACA, they are asked for a significant donation to cover the animal's care while he is being fostered. If later he is returned to PACA, he is then cared for by volunteer foster families (Long 1999). When an animal is fostered in a person's private home, personality is easily discernible and the foster caretaker can relay those traits to others.

At AHANM, animals must exhibit or appeal to workers on more distant, and at times more challenging levels. People wishing to surrender an animal at this shelter typically call first and are put on a list to reserve a cage. The workers do a cage count every morning to determine the number of available cages, and once these are filled, they start to turn away incoming animals. In most cases, clients are willing to wait an extra day or two to get their animals in, rather than take them to the city pound. Clients are also asked to make a donation towards the care and feeding of the animals, whether it is a stray or a personal pet. Many customers call and tell workers that they wish to donate their dogs. Immediately, workers explain that the animal itself is not a donation. This simple statement sets up the first construction of the animal as a subject, and not an object. The dog or cat being housed at the shelter is being provided with safe haven, and the owners are made aware that their rejection of the pet is indeed a rejection of a *subject* with far less monetary significance than emotional value.

Animals are brought in by their owners to an open area with a counter. This counter is where people adopt *and* leave pets. Cats are crated, and dogs are leashed to prevent altercations. A worker can almost immediately determine certain personality traits before the animal even crosses the threshold. As Tracy mentioned, many of the workers in the front office do not have professional animal handling experience when they start work at the shelter, but they do have what she calls a "touch" with animals. They have had previous experiences employing empathy with animals. For the safety of everyone involved, new workers and volunteers learn proper handling techniques, how to recognize adoptable traits, and how to read body language by watching more experienced workers. Tracy believes there is a difference between handling an animal in a shelter as opposed to other environments, such as training facilities and veterinarians' offices. Trainers and veterinarians see animals that have homes, and they often see them with a bonded human who can translate their behavior (Sanders 1994, 48). Animals coming in to the shelter will be left to the care of strangers who know little to nothing about that animal's experiences or reactions to stress. After enough experience, many workers can tell which animals will probably adjust and which will not. Adult cats are typically handled with extreme caution and respect, because they tend to be more dangerous and less adaptive than incoming dogs.

Tracy states that she makes an effort to establish some sort of communication with the dog as soon as it comes in. When the person bringing in the animal has little information to offer, she relies on the animal to tell her.

> I usually try to come around the desk when I can . . . talk to the animal and kind of get down on its level and look into its eyes and touch it. I think you kind of get a feeling for the kind of animal it is. Whether it has those really sweet gentle eyes, or whether it has those rambunctious "I'm ready to play" kind of eyes, whether it's jumping on you or that kind of thing. It makes you conscious of what you put in the computer because everything you put in there is going to sway not only whether someone adopts it but whether it even goes up for adoption.
>
> Sometimes I feel like the ones I spend more time with seem happier in the kennel. Some of them . . . I know they're not adoptable from the get-go. They're a spay agreement, and they're like seven months old now and they've never been on leashes and they're pooping as they come in. You have to carry them; they're ratty chow mixes, got dirt clods hanging off of them and they're terrified and they look like they're going to be fear biters. Those are the ones . . . you have a feeling they're not even going up for adoption. I honestly don't spend very much time with them. I'm not going to see them again. Maybe I can give more time to some other ones. Push your resources where it's going to do the most good. (Ploor 1999)

While individual animals can sometimes tell their own stories, numerous large litters make it more difficult for workers to determine personalities. Because communication is a two-way process, and increased levels of empathy may rely on the previous experiences of the workers, it should be obvious that certain animals also have different abilities to communicate with humans. Puppies that have been handled, walked on a leash, and allowed in the house have far better developed skills "speaking" to humans than do dogs raised in the backyard without human intervention. What Tracy was saying when she set up the previous description was that *communication is a dual process*, and some animals, based on their previous experiences, are better at it than others. Some volunteers find the attitude workers take towards litters of puppies and kittens (who have few identifiable unique traits) callous, and yet they understand this attitude when the sheer numbers of animals are explained to them. Beth was surprised by how quickly workers could decide the adoptability of puppies when she started volunteering.

> When litters come in . . . where we had six or eight identical, twin puppies, and —— was going to put half of them down before even getting to know their subtle differences. . . . I tend to think that each, well, every little being that gets here has been through so much and I don't think that it's fair to make such superficial decisions sometimes. So that really surprised me to learn how quickly those life and death decisions are made. (Petronis 1999)

Beth is a volunteer who has taken extra time to determine the cause of an animal's behavior beyond the initial interaction with the workers, who are often taking in litter after litter and animal after animal. Beth mentioned in her interview that she was also dismayed to see how little most of the staff actually interacted with the animals, though she now understands that some emotional distance is required and unavoidable. The addition of volunteers to a shelter staff allows for an attention to subtle differences between animals that is not always afforded to an actual employee. Other volunteers and some staff have protested the euthanasia criterion as it applies to individual animals, and exceptions to every rule (except overt aggression) have been made. Sometimes these exceptions are made because one or two workers or volunteers recognize special traits in an animal that other workers don't see. A flexible euthanasia system is a benefit not only to the animals, but to the morale of the workers as well. I will discuss this later, when I describe shelter policies towards pit bulls.

With owner surrenders, the worker starts by asking an owner the basics, including age, sex, and breed. Typically, owners know the age and sex of a dog, but the people who bring in strays quite often do not. A worker learns immediately how to tell if a dog has been neutered, and how old a dog is by how yellow his teeth are. Spayed females can be determined if there is a spay scar or spay tattoo, which many shelters provide as an alternative to searching for the tiny incision scars that accompany early-age spays. Once sex has been determined, gendered associations develop based on this physiological state. Intact males are often considered ill-mannered, aggressive brutes, no matter if they are tiny poodles or massive rottweilers. A lifted leg in the front office is an offense forgiven of the dog, but not the owner. When owners apologize for the behavior, workers explain that neutering would have prevented it from happening at all, and the behavior of lifting a leg to mark an unknown territory becomes an opportunity for workers to educate or chastise negligent owners. Females found with or without litters, but in various stages of lactation are treated with pity and respect for having gone through bearing and then losing a litter. These are also occasions for workers and volunteers to educate the people surrendering pets, people who could have prevented imagined suffering if they had been better prepared for pet ownership. Whether these brief lessons in pet-keeping morality are even considered by those people bringing in their pets is something that would require further study.

Workers then make an attempt to determine breed; most of the workers start work in the shelter with a basic knowledge of general breeds. They continue to refine this knowledge of breed mixes by a highly interactive process that takes place among the workers. Some have more knowledge and experience than others, and are often asked to provide their opinions when a breed cannot be determined. Typically, there are the common breed mixes that make it to shelters. In New Mexico, these are shepherds, chows, pit bulls, rottweilers, Labradors, terriers, and Australian shepherds and heelers, as well as the toy breeds, such as Chihuahuas and poodles. When I worked in Kentucky, I noticed that hounds were more common than herding breeds—a regional preference that would be affected by farming practices, geographical differences, and leisure activities in each area.

Each mix is determined by features as simple and reliable as whether or not they have a beard (terriers), a tail (Australian breeds), how flat or elongated the snout is, or coloring. Guessing breed mixes is almost a game for the workers, and a dog's breed can "change" as it progresses through the shelter, even to the point following adoption when it is seen by the adopter's veteri-

A black Labrador retriever mix at AHANM

narian. The most common of the mixes is probably the shepherd/chow mix—otherwise known to us as the "New Mexico Breed." The black, medium-sized-to-large, short-haired dogs with long tails are Lab mixes. When you work in a shelter and you have to guess the breed of twenty dogs a day, you rely on some consistent features and ignore the details. Workers rely on characteristics of about fourteen breed mixes and not eight hundred. People in various departments and volunteers will contest certain breed designations. They will be scribbled out on kennel cards and new designations written in. More timid volunteers will write "Possibly Scottie?" in the corners. Once Susan told me, "Tami, just because it's black and tan doesn't mean it's a rott-weiler!" Anything brindle is usually designated a pit bull, despite the fact that it is already long-legged, has a box-like head, and weighs about one hundred pounds at four months. Volunteers would implore us to not call anything a pit bull, stating that this breed designation would be "the Kiss of Death"!

After front office workers determine age, sex, and breed, they are required to pick names for the animals. Obviously, if the animal comes in with a name it is familiar with, that name stays, unless it is inappropriate.[1] This task swings between the front office and processing staff, and some-times serves as a point of contention between those departments. Naming animals is one of my favorite parts of the job, but other workers find it to be an incredible responsibility. Susan Brannock stated that she avoids giv-ing the animals names that mean something personal to her, for fear that this automatic connection will cause a painful loss if the animal is not adopted (she prefers to maintain some distance). Tracy believes that nam-

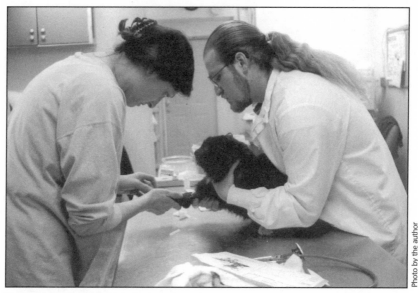

Photo by the author

Workers draw blood and vaccinate an incoming cat.

ing is an art, and should be a job for staff members who have more time to interact with the animals. She believes that being inconsiderate of an animal's personality while naming it can strongly affect the animal's adoptability. If she doesn't have time to think of a fitting name for an animal, she gives it a general name (such as "Rott" or "Black Dog") and hopes that the processing staff will later change it. Unfortunately, she has gone to the kennel to see that the dog's hastily given name remained. She feels then that no one took the time to find a better name for the animal, meaning that no one took the time to connect with it (Ploor 1999). Sylvia Taborelli commented that some of the names chosen for animals do indeed affect their adoption possibilities, such as "Limpy" or "Stinky." Usually the first words out of adopters' mouths when they see these names are "What's wrong with it?"

Animals are held in processing sometimes up to a week to determine their adoptability, and sometimes as little as a few minutes. Shy and fearful animals are often given ample opportunity to calm down, but many times being in a shelter is only more aggravating to fearfulness. During that time, employees will often allow the dogs to run around in the processing room in order to judge their level of socialization. Cats are almost always given a day or two in the intake room to calm down before they are placed in the adoption room. During that period, workers cleaning cages get some idea of the animals' personalities, and particularly noteworthy information is posted on their cage doors, such as "I'm a little scared" or "Watch Out! Escape artist!" or "I bite!" Cats that huddle behind their kitty litter boxes for more than a day or two are usually difficult to place for adoption. Dogs that try to become a part of the wall by hiding in a cor-

A cat named Aries is euthanized for a case of ringworm.

Photo by the author

ner are usually destined for euthanasia unless someone is willing to foster and rehabilitate them.

During processing, the workers vaccinate the animals, weigh them, perform a general health check, rename them if necessary, draw blood if necessary, and place them in the showing kennels. Care is taken to place dogs and cats in certain cages, even though in general all the cages appear to be the same. Females in heat are placed out of range of intact males. Excessive barkers and dog-aggressive dogs are often placed in runs with plastic dividers (the cages in the kennel are made of chain link). Hard-to-adopt animals (older or plain-featured) are placed in the first few kennels, so that they are the first and last animals adopters see when they walk in and out the door. Climbers and jumpers are given covered runs, although many are euthanized due to the belief that the average adopter will not be able to confine a particularly talented "escape artist."

Cats are also given some consideration as far as cage placement if space allows. For instance, cats of the same color are spaced out, so they do not get overlooked by customers—who might lump them all together. In addition, certain cats are noted to enjoy additional items in their cages besides the standard bowls and litter box. For instance, some cats are known to burrow, and will be given a blanket or paper bag to sleep and hide in. Such a seemingly small quirk in an animal's personality may mean the difference between adoption or euthanasia. Something as particular as the nature of a meow can affect whether a customer notices a cat. Cats are rarely moved around within the cat room, because it is believed that they prefer one cage and become upset if their environment changes too many times.

Once they make it to the kennels, the animals receive far greater interaction with other people. Customers walk through all day, volunteers come in to socialize and bathe. Those who socialize place clothespins on the cages of the animals that were walked, and they will often add comments to kennel cards to encourage people to adopt. In some cases, workers and volunteers create more elaborate signage to promote specific animals. Some of these were quite touching, as the following little poem shows.

> Poor little Peewee,
> he's just skin and bones.
> He ain't got a friend,
> he's all alone.
>
> So if you notice Peewee
> as you're walking by
> take him out and
> give him a try.
>
> You can
> take him home
> and fatten him up.
>
> Poor little Peewee
> Susan's favorite pup.
>
> (Husler 1999)

At the off-site adoption clinics, such as those held by the smaller no-kill groups, these signs were important attention-grabbers for the public. They not only gave basic information about the animal—such as breed, sex, and age—they also gave a small dramatization of the animal's history. During adoption counseling, most adopters will ask about this information, and in certain cases the stories either solicit sympathy or dramatize the victimization of the animals by humans. This gives the shelter workers an opportunity to create a feeling of sympathy or empathy between people and animals. This skill allows them to find homes for many of these dogs and cats. Newsletters and donation solicitations dramatize these stories for readers, highlighting the dignified suffering of animals, the heroics of people committed to their reha-bilitation, and the sympathy and responsibility the reader (or adopter) owes to the plight of an abandoned or abused pet. Nearly every shelter will choose a particularly moving story to send out with their donation solicitations once a year. Some organizations send these solicitations several times a year, post them on their websites, or include them in their newsletters. Once a year, PACA prints a special newsletter with a border made of pictures of all of the adopted animals that year. Sadly, these stories are not special circumstances, and the "bravery" or "dignity" of neglected and abused animals is not a rare occurrence. There are so many stories that there would be no way for any one person to tell them all. And many of them in Albuquerque are wrapped in plastic garbage bags and buried in a mass grave at the city dump.

There are animals who have unique experiences in shelters because of a conflict between how we perceive them and how they actually behave. No matter how secure we become in the knowledge of how breed, coloring, and sex affect an animal's personality, there are still groups of individuals who exhibit learned behaviors and personality traits. Some breeders and trainers suggest that even litter ranking (similar to sibling order) can strongly determine some features of a dog's personality. The following two cases will present a truly uncomfortable distinction between the experiences of individuals who are defined by common features, and how these individuals are handled within the shelter environment.

The Cultural Construction of Shelter Pets with Contested Meanings

The position of the pit bull has been a special concern of mine ever since I began this work. I don't even think I had ever consciously seen a pit bull until I moved west, where they are certainly more common than they are in Kentucky. I was curious about this, wondering if it was a regional breed preference, because it certainly is true that you see more hounds in Kentucky than you do in Albuquerque. There just isn't a lot of need for a bird dog in the desert. Why would pit bulls be a requirement for life in this desert region? Self-defense? From what or *whom?*

I believe pit bulls are more common in the Southwest because the shelters and pounds do not systematically euthanize any and all members of this breed type upon admission to the facility, as they do in Kentucky. Therefore, the dogs that we call pit bulls are allowed a multitude of individual experiences—experiences that allow them to resist the common stereotype associated with their kind. They are not limited to being guard dogs or fighting dogs (although many are certainly used for this purpose) but are successfully integrated into families and institutions. Nonetheless, there is still some discomfort over this incorporation, stemming from the strong cultural narrative about how *they are supposed to act.*

In this section, I will present some of the meanings we have constructed for the breed(s) of dog we call pit bulls. I will present the views of an English professor and dog trainer, a variety of shelter workers, government

agencies, adopters, and finally, my
own experience with pit bulls,
telling the stories of two in particular.
These two dogs had some similarities, in keeping with the designation
"pit bull," but their lives took different paths. How a cultural narrative
competes with a shelter worker's real
experience of empathy for an animal (or group of animals), and how
the workers succumb to or resist the

Photo by the author.

overriding narratives for the sake of   Marguerita, a pit bull puppy at AHANM
individual dogs are at issue.

When I started working at the shelter I learned that pit bull mix
puppies have to be the cutest puppies there are. I have a fondness for
Australian shepherds too, and those puppies are cute—but pit bulls beat
them all. Fat round bellies, with or without worms inside. Ears, posed right
on top of their head, that really have no idea what exactly their jobs are so
they stand up and fold over at their own will, sometimes at odds with each
other. Big round eyes and big square heads. Little tails that do not stop
wagging. And, yes, even puppy breath, which I am not as big a fan of as
some workers, but I could tolerate it when it was from the mouth of a little red-nose or tan-and-white pit bull.

These litters typically came in piled up in a cardboard box. Five little distended bellies, five little wagging tails, grunts and whines shooting
all that sentiment right through your rock-hard bitter soul. Many times
they were dumped somewhere. Pit bulls were popular in Albuquerque and
even though they had a "reputation," very few people could resist them
when they were cute little pups. Pups went up for adoption and they
almost always got homes.

The adults we got in ran the full spectrum of personalities, just like
other dogs. We got in smart pits and stupid pits. We got in gentlemen and
jerks. We got in sweet little matrons and airheads. We got in fighters and
lovers. We picked and chose the living from the dead based on these traits,
not based on their breed history or their "steel trap jaws." Their behaviors,
what their people told us about them, and what we could ascertain from the
look in lined brown eyes determined what sort of chance they would get.
Once, we took in a big burly neutered male with an old wound straight
down his back, ears cut close to his head, with scars and scratches. He was a

stray and we had to hold him only
a few days. We had to keep him in
isolation because he wanted to kill
every other dog he saw. He was a
"Hold Minimum," meaning that if
he wasn't claimed within four days,
he would be euthanized. After two
days a woman came in and she said
he was hers. The suspicion crept up
the back of my neck and I asked her
how in the hell he got that burn
down his back. It was obvious he
was a fighter. Could this white, mid-

A pit bull mix at AHANM

dle-class woman be fighting her pit bull? It would have blown everyone's
assumptions and stereotypes.

"I got him from Animal Control," she said. "He got those wounds
before I got him. I think he was fought. He can't stand other dogs." Ah. A
different stereotype reinforced. White, middle-class animal savior.

She was more than willing to pay the claim fees, had brought a
leash with her (which is more than most owners do) and I went back to
Isolation to spring him. I hadn't been in the cage with him before and I was
a little nervous, but as soon as I gave him my typical pit bull greeting, "Hi
Piggy!" his entire body shivered with joy and excitement. I walked right in
that cage and that sweet ninety-pound boy licked me and jumped into my
arms and let me leash him. After pulling me back to the front office, he
went home with his owner, who obviously loved him. Thankfully, she
understood his behavior; she knew how to manage his aggression, and in
doing so she saved him from himself.

Pit bulls are not a "breed" like German shepherds and Labrador
retrievers. As Vicki Hearne wrote in 1981, it is nearly impossible to describe
exactly what a "pit bull" is, besides a mix of the bulldog breeds, and that's
why breed legislation against these dogs is usually ludicrous. The executive
director at AHANM fought this breed legislation when he lived in
Colorado, and he did so by lining up several dogs and asking the judge to
identify the pit bull (Warner 1997). He couldn't, of course, because every
dog was a mix; there is no official breed called a pit bull.

Many shelters do not adopt out pit bulls or pit bull mixes. I was
very disappointed when I moved home to Kentucky for seven months and
learned that pit bulls were destroyed when they were taken to the pound or

shelter. Many people in the business seemed to oppose the ban on the breed, but no one seemed to know how to change it. I remember taking my dogs to the veterinarian and talking to the veterinary assistants about the policy of pits in Louisville and hearing them say the same thing everybody in the field there said: "Pits are great dogs, but you just can't trust the people who would adopt them. They will fight them or chain them and make them mean. It isn't worth it."

For whom? Is it truly the people we don't trust? Is this a case where the animal's individuality has once again been obliterated by the cultural narrative about the breed? Why do these "experts" deny their own knowledge and give in to popular opinion? Why are these "experts" willing to allow stereotypes to win in these cases?

Humane societies and animal control facilities play a role in this practice. Vicki Hearne made that exceptionally clear in her 1991 book *Bandit: Dossier of a Dangerous Dog*. She spends a great portion of the book trying to figure out whom to blame for the reputation pit bulls have acquired in American culture, and she directs most of the blame towards humane societies. Well, I worked at a humane society. As a matter of fact, I taught humane education. And my animal assistant was a pit bull.

The statistics support the contention that pit bulls are "dangerous" animals. According to the available sources, pit bulls have caused the highest number of dog-related fatalities in America in recent decades (only replaced by rottweilers in the last two years). This rate increased dramatically from 20 percent in 1979 to 67 percent by 1987 (Sacks et al. 1996, 891). In the cases of cross breeds, animals were counted as being part of that breed if they had one parent who was a pit bull. According to Sacks et al., out of eighty-one deaths from 1989 to 1994 where breed was known, pit bulls were involved with twenty-four of those deaths. The next most commonly reported breeds were rottweilers and German shepherds. Of all the dogs reported in fatal attacks, all but one of the males were intact. Several had a previous history of aggression (Sacks et al. 1996, 892–893).

Vicki Hearne names the humane society as the enemy of the pit bull in her exposé. She became involved in a legal case and rescued a pit mix from being destroyed. Like all dogs, if pits aren't taught manners, if they aren't taught the language of human-dog love (obedience training) and control, they are boisterous. They never learn to stop chewing the lawn furniture or jumping on the kids, so they are chained. Being chained makes them hate cats, so if they ever get off the chain, they chase down little things that move. They never learn to sit still when another dog walks by, and so if they ever get off their chain they chase down every dog they see. Sometimes those little dogs just happen to be in somebody's arms. As my friend once stated, "Just think, we bred those dogs to hate their own kind!" They need understanding and, like all pets, they require proper training. The difference between them and other breeds is the strength they possess, and the fact that the breeding of the ones commonly seen in shelters is often controlled by dog fighters. Therefore, the very traits that make them good fighters are the traits that may make them dangerous pets.

Among the animal welfare workers I documented, there seems to be an accepted idea that pit bulls are not the baby killers that the statistics and media portray. Thankfully, ever since I've worked at AHANM, they have been placed in the kennel alongside the chow and Lab and poodle mixes. This practice varies among different workers. At the time of her interview, Paula Golden could only recall placing three adult pit bulls up for adoption in her time in processing. Her thinking is this: if a pit she adopts out gets out of the yard and runs down a little old lady and her thirteen-year-old poodle, and the little old lady is bitten trying to save her poodle from the pit, Paula will have that on her conscience. And she isn't willing to take that chance (Golden 1999). Not for the dog, or the little old lady. She would rather find a home for a Lab cross or a shepherd cross and give them the cage occupied by a pit bull cross. She carries this belief because she once watched a pit grab the tail of a puppy from the other side of the chain link cage and then maul the puppy to death before she could get there to save it (Golden 1999).

Whenever I mentioned pits to Thelma Evans during our interview, she appeared to be holding back her opinion of them. Since I held her opinion in high esteem, considering that thirty years in the business might make her an expert, I finally got her to tell me her pit bull story.

> The state police had come to Ed and me several months ahead and said that they were going to do some further investigating and they would be making some arrests and they needed some place to keep the pit bulls that they brought in for evidence and they didn't trust the control center because they would be stolen or sneaked out . . . and wanted to know could and would we house them . . . we said we would do our best. . . . Nobody in the organization knew anything about it but Ed and me. So one morning, about three o'clock . . . we get a phone call here at home and said we're on our way. . . . We emptied cages, we had to double up dogs, we emptied the whole back of the kennel. . . . So here they came about daylight bringing in these dogs, some of them

bloody and some of them not. And so I forget what vet we called, it was a girl . . . and those that were injured we were trying to treat. And I was holding the dogs, and do you know she could actually take stitches, the dog would be lapping my face and she'd be stitching it up. No muzzle, no nothing. Well, they started tearing the fence apart, so we had to get sheet metal and put up between each run. They tore up the water dishes, they tore up the stainless steel, they tore up the food dishes, we'd have to stand there and take it away the minute they'd finish eating. You never saw so much activity in your life. What we went through with those pit bulls. And it went on for months. And you know in the end they were all put down but one, and this one was a champion breeder. Now the police had to give us extra protection because they were trying to break in to get their dogs. . . . Anyway, one of them took ahold of that sheet metal. . . . Another one jumped up and got ahold of the chain link and tore out a tooth. (Evans 1999)

Thelma and Ed required that the prize breeder be neutered before he was released, and the law enforcement agency agreed to honor this request. Thelma and Ed allowed the owner's veterinarian to do the surgery, and he defiantly handed the dog's testicles to the waiting police on a sponge (Evans 1999).

Vicki Hearne seems to believe that the hysteria regarding pit bulls is a class and race issue, which humane societies reinforce, and to a degree, I will agree with her. Chained pit bulls do seem to be popular in neighborhoods with high crime rates, because their reputations precede them. The common assumption about dog fighters is that they are poor, uneducated, usually inner-city or rural, and they have no regard for the suffering of others. Humane societies view these types of animals as victims of race and class, just as most of the middle class does. As Ritvo and Kete and Turner suggested in their historical treatments of the humane movement, it has been a social hygiene movement, aimed at cleaning up the lower classes, and the rhetoric is still present to this day. While humane societies may rely on some stereotypes about dogs that reinforce negative cultural stereotypes, there are real people working there who don't allow those stereotypes to keep a dog from getting a good home. I believe most shelter workers, even where the practice is banned, would support the cultural rehabilitation of pit bulls, because they know there are always exceptions to every rule. I have known two dogs that were particular exceptions to that rule.

Photo by the author.

Dogs in the kennel at AHANM

The first time I noticed Angel, I was casually walking through the kennel. I am usually drawn to the short and stout pit bull crosses, but Angel was long and lanky—almost as if she were mixed with great Dane or boxer. She was brindle, and I am not drawn to brindles as frequently as other colors. I didn't pay her much attention, thinking that she was probably not adoptable. She was a mess! You could see just about every rib she had, and her breasts were so full of milk that they practically dragged the ground.

About a week later I saw her again, but this time she was in a different kennel in a treatment cage. I stopped to look at her, somewhat amazed that she was being treated for a bacterial infection, when another worker walked by. This worker also had a soft spot for pit bulls, and as she walked past Angel she said, "We need to find her a good home. *I am not killing that dog.* I won't do it." I had only infrequently heard kennel workers state this as emphatically as she did, and from that day forward it gave me a slightly different perspective on Angel.

After Angel was in the kennel for another couple of weeks, workers in the front office decided she needed some extra promotion, and so she was taken to appear on television and special signs were posted on her cage. The signs were florescent pink, and they described her as a sweet dog that had fallen on hard luck, losing her pups and getting lost. They said that she lived up to her name and would make an excellent pet. I was touched by these pleas, but I still was not personally drawn to this rather plain, large, gangly dog.

Around the time that Angel had been there for two months, I became involved with a pilot program at the youth detention center. Several dogs would be chosen from our shelter to go and live with the children who were incarcerated there, and the kids would learn how to train and groom them. Having been involved in programs like this before, I knew it was important to pick dogs that needed extra help, but wouldn't be too difficult to place after the program was over. The trainer who was teaching the class came to the shelter to help me pick out dogs, and after he had chosen four, I made a special plea for Angel. She was a kennel favorite, I explained, but I would understand if he didn't want to use her in the program. I told him her story, and how long she had been there, and how far she had come just in those two months. I didn't necessarily do this for myself, or even for Angel. I made the effort for my co-workers, who obviously saw something in this dog that I didn't.

He took her out and we found that she was nowhere near being leash trained, barely paid any attention to either of us, and on the way back to her cage balked better than any mule. The trainer decided she would make a good example of specific training problems to the kids, and he agreed to use her. Part of me felt a bit nervous about making him choose her because this meant that she would spend three more weeks away from the shelter in another pen. I also realized that with her nondescript appearance and pendulous shrinking breasts, she might need some extra help. Training would give her an edge.

The day I transported the animals over, the two young men in the class of five immediately gravitated towards the adult dogs, while the women picked the four-month-old pups to train. The kids were actually all eighteen and over; they had completed their GEDs but were there to serve their full sentences. The young man who chose to work with Angel had introduced himself to me by explaining that his parents had kept guard dogs to protect their drugs, but that the dogs were actually quite sweet-natured to the family. He made an astute observation of Angel almost the first day he met her—he noticed that she walked sideways, and suggested that she had been chained to a cement block and had grown up pulling it behind her. That explained her sideways, gangling lope, and that was a perspective on her that I never would have thought of, having never conceived of confining a dog so harshly.

During the first training session, Angel immediately gave us a clue of her past. During one exercise, the trainer used a simple hand signal instructing her to sit. She ducked her head and moved about five feet away from him in fear. We explained to the students that this was a fear reaction, probably based on past abuse. I warned them to proceed cautiously with her and give her extra patience and time to learn these new rules. Although I maintained a calm exterior as I instructed them on her behavior, inside I was quite concerned that she might not make it through this program without biting someone.

The dogs lived at the detention center for three and a half weeks. I came to assist and lend support several times a week, and had some interesting interactions with workers at the center. One woman, when I asked her to respect the dogs' feeding schedule and not feed them extra food, asked me if I had become callous from working at the shelter for so long. Her question produced some strong feelings in me, because I was anything but callous on the inside, no matter how firm and stern I came across to outsiders. As a matter of fact, for some time I had felt like a raw wound, as if I could not make any difference at all against violence or abuse or neglect. I was overwhelmed again, and her casual comment made me wonder why I was doing this at all. While I started to question my role in this drama, Angel put on weight and filled out. About a week after she was there, she started playing more often, wrestling with the puppies and kissing the students. She often held her bowels until potty breaks, and her timid fears eased somewhat. Her trainer taught her to walk in and out of her cage willingly, instead of being dragged or pushed. Once I even saw him sweetly pick her up like a seventy-pound baby and carry her into the cage. Although I was not present for the entire time, I saw a remarkable change in her and noted it to everyone at the shelter. She had bonded especially with her trainer, and I knew that the separation was going to be difficult for both of them.

On the last day of the training, I went to pick up the dogs to take them to a special adoption clinic. I let Angel out of her cage and she bounded across the courtyard in joy at being released. I felt like a traitor to her for taking her away from this home, where she had received more attention and honor and affection than she had probably ever known. But the time had come for her to move on, for the kids to move on to the next group of dogs, and I assured them that she would find a home. Later, I sat at the adoption clinic for five hours. Despite news coverage, despite training, despite the fact that each dog was half price for spaying and neutering, vaccinations, and micro-chipping, neither of the adults found homes that day. That meant I had to take them back to the shelter.

We must keep in mind that in most cases, being housed at the shelter is a far better thing for the strays (and sometimes even the owners' pets) that come in. The alternatives are the street and the Mesa, which lies west of Albuquerque, where innumerable dangers await domesticated animals. The difference for these dogs was that I had seen a relationship develop between them and some lonely, supposedly hardened teenagers. I had seen these kids make every effort to learn new techniques of handling animals that did not involve losing their tempers or becoming frustrated. When the kids got in trouble, their first fear was that they would not be allowed to work with the dogs anymore. The empathy that may have been repressed in them because of their experiences with loved ones grew stronger as they were allowed to nurture these animals in a safe and unselfconscious environment. Both groups were injured—children and animals. Together they worked to make themselves better able to handle intimacy and trust. Angel's trainer stated that he understood, through training a dog, what his teachers and mentors in the detention center were trying to teach him: how to avoid being returned for misbehaving. I was honored to be part of a program that brought affection and love into those lives, and I felt guilty for taking it away when the session ended. There I was, bringing these poor dogs back to a noisy, crowded, lonely cement kennel, after taking them away from young men and women who said goodbye with tears in their eyes.

As I loaded them up in the car, I heard someone say, "They're probably wondering what they did wrong!" They did look confused and frightened. I held it together until I got Angel to the kennel at the shelter and she had to be picked up and deposited inside by the volunteer that was helping me that day. The time it had taken her to learn to walk into her cage didn't make a difference to her now, because she knew what life would be like again. She knew. I unhooked her leash and started crying. I knew then that my commitment to this work would have to shift towards another avenue, because the pain of seeing these creatures being rejected by strangers was too much for me to bear any longer. There was a price to pay for helping, and it felt like a huge hole in my heart.

Beth Petronis was there that day, and she told me not to worry, that we would find them homes. I nodded, knowing that everyone rallies around certain hard luck cases, and Angel certainly was one of the worst I had seen in years. I told Beth that I wasn't really worried about them being euthanized, I was more concerned about how it felt for them to be brought back to the shelter again, especially after such a fun adventure with the kids. It just didn't seem right. I kept thinking of people I had known who had once seemed so dedicated to this work telling me how happy it had made them to know that they would never again have to toss a terrified dog into a cage or put down a perfectly healthy animal for space. I knew as I knelt there on the cold cement stroking her that there was only so much I could do to help these animals and that I was nearly out of the strength and determination it took to help the next one. It was time for someone else to do this part. I was officially burned out.

As of the writing of this chapter, Angel is still housed at AHANM, awaiting a home. Just as she hangs in limbo, not knowing what the future holds, so will the ending of this part of the story. This might give you some idea of what it's like to be a dog waiting for something to happen at an animal shelter—and a worker who waits to see if someone will recognize the special traits in this animal. Even the pit bulls, despite what we think they might do to us, despite the stories we have been told about them, have their own unique stories to tell.

Perhaps Angel, and many other pit bulls, struck a chord with me because I currently live with a pit mix. She's copper and white, and when I found her I thought she was a boxer mix. Then, when her little barrel chest filled out more, and her ears flipped back instead of up, and I saw her massive adult teeth come in, I had to admit she was a pit bull. Later, I realized she probably had some Jack Russell terrier in her, because she stayed small and petite—not bulky and square like many pits. She has some black ticking on the copper parts of her, and she has a longer snout. Then again, if I hold her ears back like they've been cut, she looks remarkably like a full-blooded American pit bull terrier. I only know this because I bought a book on them. I have no idea if I have ever seen a full-blooded American pit bull terrier in the flesh. I have argued with many people about what's in her, but "pit people" recognize her for her true blood. She's a little bit ferocious when dogs get too close to her yard. Even in Kentucky, where pits are rare in the suburbs, the people who actually knew what a pit was saw it in her. I tried my best to be quiet about it when I left New Mexico.

This makes her seem exotic and mysterious and a touch dangerous. The thing is, she is a pussycat. As a matter of fact, she is afraid of pussycats; she's so gentle. She's also very lazy. Unlike most puppies, she snoozed through most of her first year of life (when she wasn't eating whatever plastic item she could find). She adores children. My mother has allowed her inside her house to play with her grandchildren, even though it took me a year to tell my mother I had adopted a pit bull. No matter, because as I've heard time and time again, "Wow, I guess it's all in how they're raised." People take one look at her narrow smiling brown eyes, obsequious posture, playful, wagging tail and immediately put their faces down for kisses. When a child enters the room, she'll keep in a down-stay and crawl to the baby in order to give her a kiss. People, including moms and dads, laugh when I tell them what she is supposed to be, but very seldom do people pull their hands or faces away. With a lick on the hand, she assures them right away that she is not going to eat them.

Photo by the author, 2000

Drew, with a wide pit bull smile.

Other than her suspicion of and hurling expletives at strange dogs, she is pure joy, a clown and a lady. She loves to dance to Patsy Cline. She loves to play hide and seek with my orange tabby. She loves to curl into a ball with her head on the floor and her butt in the air and peek at me as if I don't see her in such a ridiculous posture. She respectfully defers to my old male cat, who is now twelve years old. I adore her. I named her Drew after Nancy Drew, because I decided that any twelve-week-old puppy who would leave her house with a chain and padlock around her neck, hook up with a homeless person, be hidden in a duffel bag to ride the city bus to a drop-in center where my roommate worked so she could bring her home to me, so I could take her to the shelter was intrepid, brave, and resourceful—just like Nancy. Plus she was a strawberry blonde. Her name was Drew the second I saw her, and she never left my house again. My relationship with this dog, a dog recognized by most as a pit bull, has been a friendship, so unlike the stewardship I had with Camille. Drew came to me with her own inherent uniqueness—a uniqueness that meant I could truly enjoy her for all that she was—an individual with some quirks, but in the end, the sum of many parts that make a dog a best friend. She and I have a relationship of mutual respect; we tolerate one another because we care. Having her in my life has made me more aware of the circumstances that surround these types of dogs, and the precarious roles they play in our society.

Pit bulls are a special case because there are so many different narratives that compete to define the dogs, as I believe I have shown in this chapter. There are some that I chose to leave out, because other authors, like Vicki Hearne, have covered them in their own discussions, and the media certainly plays a role in creating a persona for these dogs. My concern is that humane societies, city councils, and insurance companies rely only on statistics and media as the primary definition of what these dogs are about, even though the workers and the dogs themselves quite often dispute the generalizations these reports document.

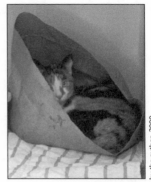

A calico cat hides in a bag in her cage at AHANM.

Photo by the author, 2000

Perhaps pit bulls (and lately rottweilers) threaten humane societies because these dogs somehow resist the narrative of animal as victim, and therefore test the limits of empathy. According to the stories Thelma and Paula told, some of these dogs are the perpetrators of violence, or seem to be not strongly affected by human intervention on their behalf. They are the animals we are protecting other animals from: baby kittens; elderly poodles; sweet little puppies. Because of their aggression, they are systematically killed in most shelters to make room for more tractable, less threatening pets. In these cases, whether they are personally aggressive or not, all of the animals associated with the breed are held responsible for the actions of a few. It is harder to feel sorry for a dog that could potentially hurt you!

However, I know from my experiences with Angel and Drew (and the acquaintance many other shelter workers have had with them) that legislation banning the breed—requiring that they be instantly euthanized in shelters and pounds—is irresponsible and inhumane, not only to those dogs, but to people as well. It obliterates the possibility of communion with individuals in order to protect some image of what a stereotype of a dog is supposed to be in our culture. If these breeds are adopted out of shelters and are allowed to have their idiosyncrasies and breed traits—just like every other breed—then perhaps they won't threaten our collective imaginations with the myth of the steel trap jaw, the time bomb, and the crazed beast devouring tiny children and little old ladies and kittens. In my opinion, pit bulls symbolize our fear of losing control over our environments, and they are that backlash harnessed by a thick chain and a spiked collar. Through the technology of domestication, they become the gargoyles of our imaginations, producing a construction of a dog that resists almost every redeeming feature of our closest relationships with another creature. They symbolize the terrible horror that happens when the chain snaps and the boundary (our control over nature or even our reliance on stereotypes) is breached—what happens when the supposed wrong people abuse nature and technology and the animal resists the myth of victimization.

Perhaps allowing them to be individuals will preserve the integrity of our bond with these misunderstood beasts. I have made it one of my personal goals to reconstruct the pit bull and I do this by taking Drew everywhere I possibly can. I never saw myself as a pit bull owner, but Drew is well trained. She is kind. She is reliable. And compared to the roller coaster of loving Camille, she is a welcome relief. She breaks down the boundaries of being a pit, but at the same time is a perfect example of what a "pit" is—a good dog! I have taken my pit to schools and conferences. I have taken her to hospitals and hotels. I will adopt pit bulls out of the shelter, and I will do it responsibly and without relying on too many stereotypes or imagined fears of horrible fates worse than death. I will have faith that I am not the only person, besides Vicki Hearne, who loves a pit bull for everything that the breed is and everything she can be. This is what humane education should be—animals teaching us lessons. Pit bulls, each and every one of them, show us that all too often our convenient cultural categories obliterate our complex social lives.

Conclusion: Fuzzy Boundaries

When people call and inquire about leaving their pets at AHANM, they often ask the workers, "How long do you give them?" The workers are trained to tell the customers that there is no set period of time for an animal in this shelter. Unlike other shelters and pounds, the animals are not given a set number of days and then euthanized randomly. A whole multitude of factors determine how long an animal will be given a cage to sleep in and a staff to tend to its basic needs. I have seen animals given five minutes, and I have seen animals that had been in the shelter system for months.

This philosophy of considering the whole picture is not unlike a philosophy that has been applied to animal rights and our relationship to our natural world by feminist philosophers. To consider the bigger picture of animal welfare and the individual experience of each animal prior to taking its life is a seemingly enormous responsibility to the outsider. Shelter workers manage this balancing act every day. There are no absolutes when it comes to animals, just as there are never absolutes when it comes to interacting with people. There is no either/or, but there is, perhaps, a possibility for both/and (Donovan 1993, 167–194). Preserving some lives over others angers many volunteers, especially when they believe personal prejudices enter into life or death judgments. My answer has always been, and will continue to be, "Of course these are subjective decisions. This is the real

world. This is how decisions are really made and how life is actually lived."
It isn't only a matter of justice, or rationality, as some philosophers might
have us believe. It is not only a matter of time being up or the ability to find
a home for the healthy ones. It is a complicated matter between a person
and an animal (and in some cases, a number of people and an animal).
When I am questioned about the decision I made to euthanize my own
dog, Camille, I do not have the ability to convey to a casual acquaintance
what her life and death meant to me. Her meaning was far too precious to
my own meaning, and I cannot yet release that very personal story from the
grips of my inner knowledge. I simply know that I made the right choice.
Everything about her story and its meaning in my life continues, beyond
her death, to have relevance. Camille's "victimhood" produced meaningful
connections which provided me, as a woman, as her caregiver, with clues
towards greater personal awareness. Her experience of abuse allowed me to
explore my own experiences of childhood suffering and subsequent control
over my social environments.

The question will probably arise, "Is shelter work a feminist activity?"
In that the work being done by animal shelters, rescue groups, sanctuaries and
other organizations celebrates and dignifies the emotional connection
between people and the natural world, in that those workers would most certainly choose the creation and support of that emotional bond over its
destruction, I would say yes. Is euthanasia an act of resistance, the act of offering release from suffering by people who know only too well what suffering
is about? It is destruction—true, but it is a destruction that is viewed as leading the way for a better life for others. It is certainly a tricky question, and I
truly do not know how to answer it. I don't appear to be alone in avoiding a
real discussion about marginalized peoples and euthanasia.

Many philosophers avoid the issue altogether, dancing around it as
they dance around the issues of human euthanasia and abortion. Killing
healthy animals in order to control population is bound by class, gender, ethnicity, religious belief, and the place of animals in individual belief systems.
I will not privilege such a question with a definitive answer (I don't think or
feel that there is one). I will say that every shelter worker would agree that
alternatives to killing, ones that don't imply future suffering for individual
animals, are desperately needed, and we must ask our neighbors to help us
find that solution. This is not a problem that shelters should have to face
alone; it is a problem found in the whole of the human community.

This is where the work of the "no-kill" shelters can be so valuable
to traditional animal sheltering, as long as those workers do not set up

oppositions to the people who make their very work possible. Killing animals has not yet passed from our American reality, and I personally prefer that it be done by caring people like the ones I met during the course of my research. They care because they know how those animals feel. There are analogs in their own experiences, and killing because they care is not always a conflict. As many of my co-workers have stated, sometimes it is the only right thing to do. I oppose philosophers who claim that some forms of death and killing are beyond the physiological or biological abilities of one gender. Like birth and pain, some forms of death are part of the cycle of all life, and many women participate in that cycle, either consciously or not.

From the moment they enter a shelter, or are introduced to a rescue worker, or are picked up from the street, animals begin a relationship with people involving communicating what it can to the person, and the person interpreting those communications and relaying them to others. In shelters and rescue groups, that communication is often tied to the dialogue of power and victimization. In some cases, a life history can be reconstructed through stories of resistance and rehabilitation. In others it is completely deconstructed through killing. There will either be a worker who cleans up after them for ten more years or a worker who cleans them up.

As I drew closer to finishing this writing, I had a dream. As I noted previously, the dreams shelter workers have are often about the loss of boundaries, about empathy so heightened that there is no physical difference between the animals and the workers.

This dream was somewhat different. The development team at the shelter wanted to work on a new marketing plan. This plan was to completely silence all of the workers at the shelter, and allow the animals to speak for themselves. As I was dreaming, I remember thinking how absurd this plan was, as most marketing plans usually seem to me, but I was voyeuristically interested to see how it would turn out. Walking through the shelter compound, the only sounds to be heard were the barks of the dogs in the kennel. The people who worked there moved around silently and wistfully, performing their duties with little joy, wanting to talk, but keeping quiet for fear that any utterance would cause them to lose their jobs. As they sprayed down kennels and cleaned out litter boxes they moved like apparitions in their royal blue scrubs, and their eyes were filled with a deep sadness.

I wrote this book to honor the selfless hard work of the dozens of people I have met who live to help animals. I felt I was also honoring the work traditions of women and other people who were not allowed to participate in the overt control of their culture and society. Much of this book has been memoirs of working in this field, and is therefore on that level self-serving and self-involved. Someone else might have written something completely different, or had a vastly unique experience with these same events. I only hope I have represented these people and animals adequately and honestly, and that I have conveyed the sense of connection I have with animals. They are some of my best friends.

The dream informed me that as an observer and a participant in this drama of sheltering companion animals, I have been afforded the role of translator/medium/filter. Empathy with animals is heightened nearly to a point of loss-of-self in this work. And it is likely that those individuals who are drawn to this work are those who have had emotional experiences similar to a dog abandoned in a shelter: separation, isolation, lack of understanding, and loss of connection. There is a great deal of sadness and resignation in welfare work after the initial joy of being surrounded by animals wears off. That resignation surfaces in different ways among individuals. Some express it with callousness, others with anger. Some neglect those feelings and present themselves as happy-go-lucky or with a display of intense sincerity. Others retreat from the work, appearing like the apparitions in the dream, floating through a forty-hour week, going through shallow motions, believing that their efforts are hardly appreciated or effective. Indeed, in my experience managers, board members, volunteers, other welfarists, and the public do not openly appreciate shelter workers.

The purpose of this book, besides providing a documentation of my observations of the institutional life of animal welfare workers, is to reify my belief that the human-animal dyad is a mutual bond, a complex social relationship of codependence and coexistence. Animals can certainly speak for themselves, but who actually listens? In these cases of abandonment and neglect, of overt abuse and negligence, it is the animal welfare workers who serve as translators for these conditions. I am not talking about the administrators, although they are certainly valuable and have often gained their positions by working their way up through the ranks. I am talking specifically about the people who clean up feces, place food in front of a starving cat, and bottle-feed babies every two hours for several weeks so that they might get a chance at a full life. These are the people who truly connect and listen to what companion animals are saying.

As I have hopefully shown, those translations are highly dependent on the life experiences of the humans who are part of the communicative exchange. These welfare workers maintain it in the middle ground, they keep the connection from being severed as an animal waits to be redefined and rehabilitated by a permanent codependent. These workers are uniquely suited to translate the needs of animals because in many cases they have also felt abandoned, neglected, hungry, and desperate for the chance to belong. In the abstract area in between definition people like Susan, Paula, Kelly, Tracy, Jane, Barbara, Thelma and the Colonel, and all of the others create worth and value for the lives of animals like Angel, Charley, Hank, Sunshine, and Aries—lives that are in between belonging, but still have value and significance.

I worked in this field and wrote these stories so that some of those bonds would never be broken. Even in those cases where the individual is superceded by the ideal, names are remembered. Odd little habits or unique markings, beautiful meows or howls can make one black cat or plain-looking shepherd mix the most interesting animal in the kennel. I will always remember that great Dane who was surrendered after his owner died. I was sitting in a cage with him and Paula and when she reached over to read his tags, his ears went back and his teeth were bared and I nearly lost it before I made it out of the cage. Once I could safely look back at Paula, we both started to laugh because she couldn't believe I could move so fast. When the massive dog was finally sedated in order to handle him, he lost his own urine out of his terror. I stood outside the cage for long time staring at that spot on the kennel floor, a pool of urine that said so much about what had happened to his life since his human companion had abandoned him in death.

I can remember a cat named Harry that would follow me around the cat room while I cleaned up after all the other animals. Harry was somehow intellectually above cage confinement, he seemed perfectly content to hang out and muse over his current state of living. Harry was eventually adopted by a young couple who found that he even enjoyed car rides. Another little orange tabby, whose name I don't remember now (perhaps his name isn't the important part of his story), would immediately wrap his arms around your neck when you opened his cage, and rub his mouth so furiously against your cheeks and lips that you were soon covered in cat saliva. He would madly purr through this display of friendship, and I have hardly ever been so moved and tickled to make the acquaintance of a cat. He seemed to forget that I was a person and not a cat—and for a brief time I was filled with joy that a cat was speaking to me in his own language, and that I recognized the language as one of belonging, affection, and acceptance.

Every single worker and volunteer can think of some special animal who spoke to them; one who communicated terror or anger, or in the better cases, joy and friendship. Sometimes, animals were somehow able to convey gratitude. It doesn't matter to the people who work in a shelter if some scientists dispute that a wagging tail or a contented sigh means "thank you" or not. So much of the communication between a welfare worker and an animal happens only between those two individuals, and in verbal silence. The momentary bond two strangers make in shelters could very well determine the course of both of their lives. The people will take a "thank you" however they can get it.

There was one instance of animal resistance that I will never forget, one animal that spoke—using *my* language, actually spoke—and put so many of these conflicted feelings into a simple statement for me. I was assisting three workers with euthanasia. Two of us were working in one area, while the other two workers were killing animals in another part of the same room. They brought in a skinny, wild, black Lab cross. He had to be under a year—they could hardly hold him still to inject him, and as they did it he barked and squirmed the entire time. I glanced over at them during a break between our animals and thought they had finally managed to inject him. As one of them snapped opened a garbage bag, the dog suddenly let out two final barks. We all stopped what we were doing and looked at him, while one of them listened through a stethoscope for a heartbeat. Dogs do not typically bark after the sodium pentobarbital is fully injected. After they were sure his heart had stopped beating, the workers grinned at me and praised him for mouthing off.

"Did he say what I think he said?" I asked gleefully.

One of them smiled and said, "Sounded like he said 'Fuck you!'"

We laughed and gave him a cheer and agreed that we were the most awful people on the Earth, and that we deserved to be cussed out by that truly obnoxious, plain-looking, frightened dog that was being killed because he didn't fit in. I have seen literally thousands of black Lab mixes killed since 1996 when I started volunteering at the animal shelter. Even to the last moment, we recognized that this one would resist our efforts to "construct" his experience for him—he decided to leave us with a nagging doubt and a reminder that we do not have absolute control. I will never forget that dog.

Over the course of the year after I put Camille to sleep, I had several dreams about her. In those dreams, I would be somewhere in my apartment, performing some insignificant daily chore, and she would come scampering into the room accompanied by the other dogs. She would have that wide grin on her pointed little face and her eyes would twinkle as she came running to me for a pat on the head. Each time I had this dream, I would shake my head in amazement that she was back. "No, no," I would tell her, "You're gone! I had to kill you last year!" I would awake from the dream feeling guilty and then frustrated that I had not resolved my guilt. Then I had a dream about her where I was lying in bed and once again she came running in from another room. I told her to leave me alone, but she hopped into bed and snuggled up next to me. Instead of having a sleek, shiny black coat, she was matted and dull. Her eyes weren't twinkling the way I remembered them, instead they were clouded and out of focus. She was panting hard, and her stub of a tail didn't wiggle like it used to when she saw me. I told her she had to stop coming to see me. I didn't deserve to be haunted by her.

Then I realized what I was doing. I realized that she wasn't haunting me in order to shadow my decision with blame or accusations. She was resisting my expectations of what causing her death would mean to me. She did not fulfill my rescue narrative, she was not rehabilitated and made whole through her association with me. In the dreams, she was visiting me, making sure that I did not forget how lovely and devoted she was. And each time I pushed her away, I denied her memory and broke the bond we had. I denied that, for all intents and purposes, she was me, and I was rejecting that part of me that she was. That was why she appeared to me in such a forlorn state in the last dream. Just as I could not deny how my story became hers, neither could I deny that in many ways, she wrote her own story. She refused to be incorporated or constructed according to my expectations. Her visit in my dream reminded me of the lasting impression her life made on mine, the lesson of life that she taught me.

Notes

Chapter One: Camille's Story

1. There is, of course, the possibility that people are drawn to this work because of ineffective relationships to people in their lives, and are therefore preselected. Exploration of these issues might be interesting in terms of psychological profiling. Harold Herzog (1993) interviews a number of animal activists and finds a number of similarities among them regarding similarities in the process of incorporation.

Chapter Four: "This One Mattered to Me . . . "

1. As a side note, when I began Kelly's interview we met at an adoption clinic. When I turned on the tape recorder, her first comment was that someone had just asked her if they could unspay a dog.

2. Another work that traces one woman's involvement in rescue work is Terri Crisp and Samantha Glen's *Out of Harm's Way* (1996). She got involved with her local shelter while searching for her missing cats.

3. It is commonly accepted among welfare workers that "farm people" keep animals outside, in keeping with a working animal or livestock, while urban people are more likely to treat them as pseudo-family members and let them in the house. This does not imply that "farm people" are more likely to mistreat animals, simply that they have a different relationship with their pets. It only becomes a problem for workers when a person from a rural background moves to an urban environment and either allows an animal to run loose, or chains it instead of providing it with an enclosure.

4. Including myself. Shortly after completing this research, I resigned from my position at AHANM. One outcome of "going native" while also attempting to maintain the pursuit of higher education was that I became seriously indebted and had to forfeit my career in this field to afford to live comfortably. This is an aspect of research not often discussed by academics, but should be.

Chapter Five: Bridging the Bond

1. One time a pit bull came in named "Penis," and that name was obviously changed. If there are already too many animals in the kennel with the same name ("Baby" is one of the most common), workers will change it to something that sounds similar, or add a number to the end of the name (i.e., "Baby 1," "Baby 2").

References

Adams, Carol J. 1994. "Bringing Peace Home: A Feminist Philosophical Perspective on the Abuse of Women, Children, and Pet Animals." *Hypatia* 9: 63–84.

Albuquerque Animal Control Ordinance. 1999. City of Albuquerque: Environmental Health Department, Animal Control Division.

Andes, Ramon. 1999. Personal communication with the author.

Arluke, Arnold. 1994. "'We Build a Better Beagle': Fantastic Creatures in Lab Animal Ads." *Qualitative Sociology* 17: 143–158.

Arluke, Arnold, and Clinton R. Sanders. 1996. *Regarding Animals*. Philadelphia: Temple University Press.

Baca, Cynthia. 1999. Interview with the author.

Beard, K. Rutledge. 1999. Personal communication with the author.

Beck, Alan, and Aaron Katcher. 1996. *Between Pets and People: The Importance of Animal Companionship*. 2d ed. West Lafayette, IN: Purdue University Press.

Boyer, Jim. 1965. "Shelter Conditions Show Improvement." *Albuquerque Tribune*, 15 January, 1–2.

———. 1965. "City Center Rarely Treats Animals." *Albuquerque Tribune*, 9 July, 12.

———. 1965. "Surprise Pound Inspections Barred by a New Entryway." *Albuquerque Tribune*, 24 April, 9.

Brannock, Susan. 1999. Interview with the author.

Branning, Don. 1967. "It Takes Nerve to Tell People That They Are Cruel to Animals." *Albuquerque Tribune*, 1 July.

Britton, Marcy. 1999. Interview with the author.

Buettinger, Craig. 1997. "Women and Antivivisection in Late Nineteenth-Century America." *Journal of Social History* 30: 857–872.

Camille Claudel. 1990. Dir. Bruno Nuytten. Perf. Isabelle Adjani and Gerard Depardieu.

Camitta, Miriam. 1990. "Gender and Method in Folklore Fieldwork." *Southern Folklore* 47: 21–32.

Chapel, Kelly. 1999. Interview with the author.

DiGiacomo, Natalie, Arnold Arluke, and Gary Patronek. 1998. "Surrendering Pets to Shelters: The Relinquisher's Perspective." *Anthrozoös* 11: 41–51.

Donovan, Josephine. 1993. Animal Rights and Feminist Theory. In *Ecofeminism: Women, Animals, and Nature,* edited by Greta Gaard. Philadelphia: Temple University Press.

Dowling, Julie Miller. 1998. "Unwanted Burden: Animal Shelters Debate the Role of Euthanasia." *HSUS News,* Winter.

Dunlop, Robert H., and David J. Williams. 1996. *Veterinary Medicine: An Illustrated History.* St. Louis: Mosby.

Ehn, Jack. 1979. "Animal Shelter Probe Results in Resignations." *Albuquerque Tribune,* 7 July, 1, 8.

Evans, Thelma. 1999. Interview with the author.

Finsen, Lawrence, and Susan Finsen. 1994. *The Animal Rights Movement in America: From Compassion to Respect.* New York: Twayne Publishers.

Francione, Gary. 1996. *Rain without Thunder: The Ideology of the Animal Rights Movement.* Philadelphia: Temple University Press.

Gates, Barbara T., and Ann B. Shtier. 1997. *Natural Eloquence: Women Reinscribe Science.* Madison, WI: University of Wisconsin Press.

Golden, Paula. 1999. Interview with the author.

Graeme, Jack. 1969. "Most Popular Pup in City Mends as Money Rolls In." *Albuquerque Journal,* 15 March, 1.

Hall, Mike. 1999. Interview with the author.

Haraway, Donna. 1989. *Primate Visions.* New York: Routledge.

———. 1991. *Simians, Cyborgs, and Women.* New York: Routledge.

———. 1992. "The Promises of Monsters: A Regenerative Politics for Inappropriate/d Others." In *Cultural Studies,* edited by Lawrence Grossberg et al. New York: Routledge.

Harbolt, Tami. 1999. "Inside the Shelter: Ethnography and the Human-Animal Bond." Paper presented at Going Native: Recruitment, Conversion, and Identification in *Cultural Research.* Center for Folklife Studies at Ohio State University, Columbus, OH, May 20–22.

Harding, Sandra. 1991. *Whose Science? Whose Knowledge? Thinking from Women's Lives.* Ithaca: Cornell University Press.

Hearne, Vicki. 1982. *Adam's Task: Calling Animals by Name.* New York: Vintage Books.

———. 1991. *Bandit: Dossier of a Dangerous Dog.* New York: Harper Perennial.

Herzog, Harold. 1993. "The Movement Is My Life: The Psychology of Animal Rights Activism." *Journal of Social Issues* 49: 103–119.

Hess, Elizabeth. 1988. *Lost and Found: Dogs, Cats, and Everyday Heroes at a Country Animal Shelter.* New York: Harcourt, Brace, and Company.

Humane Society of the United States Animal Services Consultations Preliminary Report, Resulting from the HSUS May 15th–17th Visit, 6 June 2000.

Husler, Susan. 1997. Interview with the author.

Kete, Kathleen. 1994. *The Beast in the Boudoir: Pet Keeping in Nineteenth-Century Paris.* Berkeley: University of California Press.

Kelber, William J. 1973. "Is Animal Overpopulation a Veterinary Problem?" *Veterinary Economics,* 26–30.

Keller, Evelyn Fox. 1985. *Reflections on Gender and Science.* New Haven: Yale University Press.

Lansbury, Coral. 1985. *The Old Brown Dog: Women, Workers, and Vivisection in Edwardian England.* Madison, WI: University of Wisconsin Press.

Lawrence, Elizabeth Atwood. 1982. *Rodeo: An Anthropologist Looks at the Wild and the Tame.* Knoxville: University of Tennessee Press.

———. 1986. "Human Perceptions of Animals and Animal Awareness: The Cultural Dimension." In *Advances in Animal Welfare Science 1985,* edited by Michael W. Fox. Boston: Martinus Nijhoff Publishers.

Lewis, Susie. 1999. Interview with the author.

Lockwood, Randall. 1995. "Anthropomorphism Is Not a Four-Letter Word." *Social Research.*

Long, Jane.1999. Interview with the author.

Lopez, Rebecca. 1966. "Thousands of Wagging Tails: Animal Shelter Load Grows." *Albuquerque Journal,* 20 November.

Lorrin, Julie.1999. Interview with the author.

Maehle, Andreas-Holger. 1994. "Cruelty and Kindness to 'Brute Creation': Stability and Change in the Ethics of the Man-Animal Relationship, 1600–1850." In *Animals and Human Society,* edited by Aubrey Manning and James Serpell. London: Routledge.

McCrea, Roswell C. 1910. *The Humane Movement: A Descriptive Survey.* New York: Columbia University Press.

McLachlan, Sarah. 1997. "Angel." *Surfacing.* Arista Records.

McNutt, Mike. 1998. Interview with the author.

Mechling, Jay. 1989. "'The Banana Cannon' and Other Folk Traditions between Human and Nonhuman Animals." *Western Folklore* 48: 312–323.

National Humane Shoptalk. 1970, January.

Newkirk, Ingrid. 1991. "Dark Angels and Direct Action." Paper presented at the conference of the Association of Veterinarians for Animal Rights and International Society for Animal Rights.

Norwood, Vera. 1993. *Made from This Earth: American Women and Nature.* Chapel Hill: University of North Carolina Press.

Padgett, Mike. 1970. "Humane Assn. Pair Answers Sharp Critics of Programs." *Albuquerque Journal,* 15 March, C-6.

Patronek, Gary, Lawrence Glickman, Alan M. Beck, George McCabe, and Carol Ecker. 1996. "Risk Factors for Relinquishment of Dogs to an Animal Shelter." *Journal of the American Veterinary Medical Association* 209: 572–581.

Peek, Charles W., Nancy J. Bell, and Charlotte C. Dunham. 1996. "Gender, Gender Ideology, and Animal Rights Advocacy." *Gender & Society* 10: 464–478.

Petronis, Beth. 1999. Interview with the author.

Ploor, Tracy. 1999. Interview with the author.

Radner, Joan, and Susan Lanser. 1993. "Strategies of Coding in Women's Cultures." In *Feminist Messages: Coding in Women's Folklore,* edited by Joan Radner. Urbana: University of Illinois Press.

Regan, Tom. 1983. *The Case for Animal Rights.* Berkeley: University of California Press.

Ritvo, Harriet.1986. *The Animal Estate: The English and Other Creatures in the Victorian Age.* Cambridge, MA: Harvard University Press.

Rollin, Bernard. 1989. *The Unheeded Cry: Animal Consciousness, Animal Pain, and Science.* Oxford: Oxford University Press.

Rosaldo, Renato. 1984. "Grief and the Headhunter's Rage: On the Cultural Force of Emotions." In *Text, Play and Story: The Construction and Reconstruction of Self and Society,* 1983, Proceedings of the American Ethnological Society. Washington, D.C.: The American Ethnological Society.

Rowan, Andrew N., and Jeff Williams. 1997. "The Success of Companion Animal Management Programs: A Review." *Anthrozoös* 1: 110–122.

Rowan, Andrew. 1997. "Shelters and Pet Overpopulation: A Statistical Black Hole." *Anthrozoös* 5: 140–143.

Sacks, J. J., R. Lockwood, J. Hornreich, and R.W. Sattin. 1996. "Fatal Dog Attacks, 1989–1994." *Pediatrics* 97: 891–895.

Sanders, Clinton R. 1994. "Biting the Hand That Feeds You: Encounters with Problematic Patients in a General Veterinary Practice." *Society and Animals* 2: 47–66.

Schiebinger, Londa L. 1989. *The Mind Has No Sex? Women in the Origins of Modern Science.* Cambridge: Harvard University Press.

———. 1993. *Nature's Body: Gender and the Making of Modern Science.* Boston: Beacon Press.

Schimkat, Helga. 2000. Interview with the author (email).

Shultz, William J. 1924. *The Humane Movement in the United States, 1910–1922.* New York: Columbia University Press.

Singer, Peter. 1975. *Animal Liberation: A New Ethics for Our Treatment of Animals.* New York: Avon Books.

Taborelli, Sylvia. 1999. Interview with the author.

Tanner, Sindy. 1999. Interview with the author.

Taxpayers' Anti-Cruelty Federation of New Mexico, Inc. 1966. Newsletter, October.

Tellier, Barbara. 1999. Interview with the author.

Trinh, Minh-Ha. 1989. *Woman, Native, Other: Writing Post-coloniality and Feminism.* Bloomington: Indiana University Press.

Tuan, Yi Fu. 1984. *Dominance and Affection: The Making of Pets.* New Haven: Yale University Press.

Turner, James. 1980. *Reckoning with the Beast: Animals, Pain, and Humanity in the Victorian Mind.* Baltimore: Johns Hopkins University Press.

Walaski, Nichoel. 1999. Interview with the author.

Warner, Joel. 1997. Interview with the author.

Williams, Patricia. 1991. *The Alchemy of Race and Rights.* Cambridge: Harvard University Press.

Newspaper References

Albuquerque Journal. 1947. "Dozen Criticisms of Dog Pound Made by Humane Association." 12 July, 5.

———. 1947. "Raps Dog Pound, Urges New One." 19 September, 4.

———. 1947. "Tag Day Today for Humane Assn." 15 November, 1.

———. 1948. "Humane Assn. Approves Action of Directors." 24 March, 11.

———. 1948. "Court Asked to Decide between Two Sets of Offices for Humane Group." 20 May, 4.

———. 1948. "City Balks on Animal Shelter." 12 May, 1.

———. 1949. "Dog Licensing to Be Enforced to Aid Fund-Short Shelter." 26 June, 1–2.

———. 1969. "Award Goes to Dog Tossed Four Floors." 13 November, E-1.

——. 1970. "Charges AHA Prejudice toward Cats." 25 March, 5.

——. 1979. "Animal Control Center Field Supervisor Is Fired." 13 July, A-3.

Albuquerque Tribune. 1947. "Animal Welfare Meet Scheduled Tonight." 18 April, 9.

——. 1947. "Animal Shelter Group Formed." 19 April, 5.

——. 1947. "Humane Group to Recruit Members." 29 August, 3.

——. 1948. "'Filigree Work' Animal Shelter Unneeded, Humane Official Says." 17 March, 4.

——. 1948. "Reaction Varies on Shelter Fund." 24 March, 4.

——. 1948. "Court Asked to Settle Arguments on Humane Association Officers." 19 May, 6.

——. 1948. "Animal Shelter Nears Completion." 27 December, 10.

——. 1949. "Animal Shelter to Open March 15." 26 February, 3.

——. 1949. "Animal Shelter to Be Dedicated." 6 April, 2.

——. 1949. "184 Dog Licenses Sold in Two Days." 4 August, 1.

——. 1949. "Dog Bites Fewer Since Shelter Opened Here." 2 September, 1.

Albuquerque Tribune. 1952. "Do You Want to Own a Dog for a Pet? Animal Shelter Has 35 Now." 26 February, 11.

——. 1956. "Animal Shelter Gets New Worker." 18 January, 2.

——. 1956. "Compromise Is Reached in Rabies Shots Proposal." 22 February, 21.

——. 1956. "Animal Protective Society Merges with Humane Assn." 7 March, A-3.

——. 1956. "City Commission Puts Off Action on Rabies Shot, Can Pool Proposal." 7 March 6, 6.

——. 1957. "Open Hearing Ordered in Shelter Fees." 19 March, 1–2.

——. 1957. "Mrs. Woolston Lauds Animal Shelter Head." 21 March, 2.

——. 1957. "Engel Will Get Animal Shelter Report Monday." 23 March, 2.

——. 1957. "Humane Assn. Directors Censure Vice President." 25 March, 1.

——. 1957. "Humane Assn. to Meet Amid Controversy." 3 April, 2.

——. 1957. "Attorney Says Humane Assn. Ouster Illegal." 4 April, 1.

——. 1957. "Humane Assn. Board Ousted in Noisy Meet." 4 April, 34.

——. 1957. "McCahon Made Offer in Veterinary Work." 6 April, 2.

——. 1957. "Humane Assn. Controversy Enters Court." 9 April, 1–2.

——. 1957. "Rouse Expects Improvements at Shelter." 27 April, 1.

——. 1957. "Humane Assn. Ouster from Shelter Sought." 3 May, 1–2.

——. 1957. "Move to Oust Advisory Board Gets Backing." 4 May, 2.

———. 1957. "Dr. Woolston Dies of Heart Ailment." 10 May, 1.

———. 1957. "Fight Looms over Ouster of Rouse." 11 May, 1–2.

———. 1957. "Rouse Ouster Hearing Opens before Board." 13 May, 1–2.

———. 1957. "Rouse Denies Charges on Animal Shelter." 17 May, 1–2.

———. 1965. "Says Many Not Told Pets Impounded." 5 May.

———. 1966. "Group Says It Will Fight Cruelty." 4 June, A-4.

———. 1968. "Anti-Cruelty Unit in Danger of Going Broke Aiding Animals." 17 April, F-5.

East Heights News. 1968. "Adoption Center for Pets Now Operates in City." 21 March.

———. 1967. "City Urges Birth Control: for Pets." 26 January.

National Humane Shoptalk. 1970. "Charlie Black Takes On Shelter Mascot Chores." 18: 1.

Index